MORE MEMORI
HUDDERSFI

TRUE NORTH BOOKS
DEAN CLOUGH
HALIFAX
HX3 5AX
TEL 01422 344344

THE PUBLISHERS WOULD LIKE TO THANK THE FOLLOWING COMPANIES FOR SUPPORTING THE PRODUCTION OF THIS BOOK

FRED BEARDSELL & SON
R BUTTERWORTH & SON LIMITED
CLIFFE & COMPANY LIMITED
CROWTHER & SHAW LIMITED
F DRAKE & COMPANY OF GOLCAR LIMITED
THE ENGLISH CARD CLOTHING COMPANY LIMITED
GARRARDS (HUDDERSFIELD) LIMITED
HANSON TRANSPORT LIMITED
HOLSET ENGINEERING COMPANY LIMITED
MITRE SPORTS INTERNATIONAL LIMITED
MOORHOUSE & BROOK LIMITED
FRANK PLATT ELECTRICAL LIMITED
QUARMBY & SYKES LIMITED
JOHN QUARMBY & SON LIMITED
SELLERS & COMPANY (HUDDERSFIELD) LIMITED
SHAW SON & GREENHALGH LIMITED
BENJAMIN SHAW & SONS LIMITED
SHAW & HALLAS LIMITED
THE UNIVERSITY OF HUDDERSFIELD
WOOD AUTO FACTORS LIMITED

First published in Great Britain by True North Books
Dean Clough
Halifax HX3 5AX
1997

ISBN 1 900 463 26 1

Introduction

The publication of our first book, *Memories of Huddersfield,* met with a tremendous response from the people in the town. Thousands of copies of the original book have been sold to date, with many finding their way overseas to bring pleasure to former Huddersfield residents who have emigrated. The letters of encouragement and kind comments we received urged us to produce a second book, this time containing even more of the excellent photographs which have provided such enjoyment. The compilation of *More Memories of Huddersfield* has been carried out over a period of several months. We always expected it to be a pleasurable experience, but in the event the satisfaction we have derived from studying the marvellous old photographs went far beyond our expectations.

Fancy dress competition at Rawthorpe Childrens' Field Day, 1953.

Increasingly, *nostalgia* is enjoyed by a growing band of people and the book is intended to appeal to a wide audience. Where possible we have tried to concentrate upon a period within the memory of most of our readers; the 1950s, '60s and '70s - decades which saw tremendous developments in the town, and a time when changes in the world of work, entertainment, public health and retailing were at their peak. *Change* takes place constantly in every town and Huddersfield is no exception. As we all get older it is often easier to 'step back' and view events and developments with a clearer sense of perspective. Our aim has been to assist in this respect by presenting a 'catalyst' capable of rekindling memories of days gone by in an entertaining manner. Looking through the pages of this book it may be surprising how much change has taken place, and over such a comparatively short period, relative to the long history of the area. Several of Huddersfield's best known and longest established firms have allowed us access to their extensive internal archives. This has enabled us to recount the history of these companies, from humble beginnings to, in most cases, leading positions in their chosen area of expertise. Of course, these organisations have tremendous social, as well as commercial significance, as between them they represent the places of employment for thousands upon thousands of Huddersfield people. We are grateful for the co-operation and support of the directors of these businesses for adding to the quality and interest of this book.

Many different aspects of life in Huddersfield are covered. Royal visits to the town are particularly memorable to most folk and we are pleased to be able to include several outstanding scenes from happy royal occasions. The world of local entertainment is covered too, with high quality pictures of former cinemas and public houses from days gone by securing a place on the following pages. Home-made entertainment, such as the events at Greenhead Park, which had been organised in wartime and continued after the end of the war, are featured too. On the same theme we have included scenes from various local carnivals processions and galas. Many of the children seen in these photographs will be reaching retirement age now and we would be pleased to hear from readers who may have recognised themselves.

Street scenes are not neglected. Photographs of this nature were popular in the last book, and understandably so. The changing face of the town is reflected in the way our roads and shops have developed to meet the changing needs of our lives over the years. These photographs show the shops and motorcars we remember from our early days, along with the fashions which were all the rage when we were younger. All combine to refresh our memories of days gone by, and when that occurs the book will have achieved its aim.

The work involved in compiling this book really has been a *labour of love* for us. Huddersfield is a marvellous town, a great place to live with much to be proud of. We hope that our feelings of pride and passion for the town come across in the following pages, and that you enjoy reading *More Memories of Huddersfield* as much as we enjoyed creating it.

Mark Smith and Phil Holland
Publishers

TEXT
PHIL HOLLAND
MORRIS BRAY
PAULINE BELL

DESIGN
MARK SMITH
MANDY WALKER

BUSINESS DEVELOPMENT
ANDREW HALES

Contents

The Southgate showroom of C.H Mitchell's Morris dealership looks marvellous in this 1953 photograph, taken to celebrate its opening. The Union flag probably owes its position here to the recent coronation of Queen Elizabeth. Classic car enthusiasts would drool over a collection of cars and vans like this if it were possible to see one today. It really is the quality of the photograph, looking as it does as if it had been taken only yesterday, that brings the scene to life. Yet this is how the cutting edge of motoring appeared nearly half a century ago. In amongst the neatly arranged flowers there are various items of motoring nostalgia, including 'Redex' the fuel additive, 'Bluecol', Duckham's oil and 'Petro-flex' flexible fuel lines. Some of these products are still available and all add character to the picture.

Events

Above: Along the route taken by the royal visitors, a Triumph *twin* is seen on stand-by as the motorcade approaches. This police officer looks a bit anxious. The photographer tells us that the Triumph motorcycle was brand new and this was its first day in service. Crowds of children, most with a Union Flag to wave, waited patiently in the bright July sunshine. As the royal cars came into view there was a shrill cheer from the loyal supporters and police officers looked on to ensure that the crowds stayed well back.

Left: Prince Charles was born in November 1948, approximately a year after his parents were married. Their wedding came just four months after the announcement of their engagement, to much public acclaim. This picture dates from July 1949 and features some of the staff at the Leeds Road ICI works who obviously had a goodwill message for Princess Elizabeth and her eight month old baby.

Right: Princess Street was the location for this scene dating from 1949. The photograph was taken to commemorate the visit of HRH Princess Elizabeth and Prince Philip to the Town Hall. The *old* Fire Station with its distinctive tall wooden doors is seen on the right. Members of the Guard of Honour, provided by the Duke of Wellington's Regiment can be seen following the military band. Interestingly, they are marching with bayonets fixed. They must have formed a memorable impression on the crowds who had turned out to watch the royal visit. The 'Special' bus parked along Princess Street would have brought passengers into town for the visit. No doubt several hundred Halifax folk would have made the journey 'over the hill' to add their support to the rousing welcome given to the future Queen.

Left: It was all getting a little too much for these Royalists on the occasion of the 1949 royal visit. The little girls (and one or two *big* girls too!) found it necessary to sit down for a while to take the weight off their feet during the warm July sunshine.

Ideal
Fountain Pen.
W H COOK
PRINTERS
STATIONERS
BOOKBINDERS
PENS
FRED BUDGE
FANCY GOODS
POUCHES
PIPES
FRED
BUDGE
HIGH CLASS
TOBACCONIST
PLAYER'S NUMBER 3
WILLS's

It was 'quick march' along Market Street for these participants in the Civic Parade, watched by youngsters from the Scouts and Guides who look rather less than impressed by the proceedings! The photograph was taken on a Sunday in May 1953. The Mayor can be seen around 15 feet behind the Mace Bearer. The formality of the occasion is demonstrated by the number of wigs and top hats being worn by the marchers. Sunday newspapers are being sold by the side of the bank, near the traffic lights. One of the posters encourages sales with the news that the paper carries 'Rommel's own story.' On the left of the picture is Fred Budge's *high class* tobacconists' shop, complete with canvas sun shade to protect his stock of pipes, lighters and tobacco products. Above the shop are the offices of W. H Cook, the long established Huddersfield printers, stationers and bookbinders. In a matter of weeks after this photograph was taken it would be the turn of a national ceremony involving a far greater degree of ancient ritual and formality. Her Majesty Queen Elizabeth II would be crowned in Westminster Abbey by the Archbishop of Canterbury on June 2nd. After the ceremony the new Queen made her way to Buckingham Palace in the gold state coach - accompanied by cheering crowds, many of whom had waited up all night to see her.

Above: Princess Elizabeth shakes hands with local dignatories during the 1949 visit. She was accompanied by the Mayoress of Huddersfield at the time, Miss Shirley Cartwright, the daughter of the Mayor Alderman David Cartwright. The future Queen looks radiant and relaxed as she meets the local officials, watched over by the stern police officers charged with protecting her. The degree of security appears modest by today's standards, with members of the public allowed to get close to the Princess to take the pictures they would treasure forever.

Right: Our intrepid photographer was positioned in a second-floor window on New Street in order to capture this scene which dates from 1949. It shows the royal motorcade as it progresses slowly down towards Market Place, flanked by mounted police officers and cheered by thousands of loyal royalists. Every vantage point was occupied by people eager to catch a better view of Princess Elizabeth (as she was in 1949) and Prince Philip. The royal couple travelled in an open-topped Daimler with officials following in a second Daimler behind. The leading and rear vehicles were police cars, each linked by radio to the senior officers charged with keeping the couple secure on their visit to Huddersfield. The street was highly decorated with Union flags and bunting, and most of the children had a flag to wave as the dignified black cars made their way up the street. Press reports from the time describe how people had arrived on the street up to four hours before the procession came through, in the hope of securing the best possible view. A wave of emotion passed along the street as word came that the royal cars were about to drive along, followed closely by cheers as the first car came into view.

Smaller picture: The long wait was rewarded when the royal Daimler came into view on the occasion of the royal visit in 1949. Heavy wooden barriers kept the crowds at bay but that didn't prevent them shouting and cheering as the future Queen approached. Some of the waiting soldiers - note how they are totally unarmed - can be seen taking a crafty sideways glance at the VIPs as the cars get closer. It would be a day that everyone here would remember for the rest of their lives.

BURTON
BURTON

EXAMINER

Left: A stern-faced Prince Philip, bowler hat in hand, confidently strides along the ranks of the immaculately turned out Guard of Honour on the royal visit of 1949. The soldiers were members of the Duke of Wellington Regiment, many of whom had clearly seen active service in the last war judging by the medals being worn. The old Examiner office can be seen on the left of the picture with its bold lettering carved into the stonework and elegant balcony above the entrance. Further down the street we can see the Art Gallery and Theatre Royal. The whole street was decked out in bunting and cheering crowds lined the route taken around the town by the royal party.

Below: Another view of the royal party arriving at the Town Hall, this time taken by Maurice Bray standing on the low wall outside the building. The Royal Standard can be seen flying on the lead limousine of the motorcade. The Mayor of Huddersfield, Alderman Cartwright, can be seen on the right of the Princess, with his back to the camera. Behind the mayor is the mace bearer, and to the right, with hands characteristically clasped behind him, is Prince Philip.

Above: The Guard of Honour forming up opposite the Town Hall in Ramsden Street during the 1949 royal visit. Crowds packed tightly behind the heavy wooden barriers and bunting blowing in the warm breeze overhead. The sound of a hundred soldiers' boots on the tarmac would have been rousing and evocative for the people gathered to see the future Queen. Memories of the war, and of loved ones who never returned from it, were fresh in their minds.

Right: The long wait to see Princess Elizabeth and Prince Philip had obviously taken its toll on some of the little girls in this picture! The picture gives an atmospheric insight into the fashions of the day; most of the children seen here had been born and brought up in the war and so were used to *making do and mending.* None of your expensive training shoes and tracksuits in those days of course.... and weren't we all better for it!

Princess Elizabeth and the rest of the royal party visited Learoyd Brothers. They were accompanied by Alderman D. Cartwright the Mayor and his daughter, Shirley. She is seen walking alongside Prince Philip as they leave the premises of the local firm. The excitement on the faces of the factory workers illustrates just how popular Princess Elizabeth was. The ladies in particular look enthralled, regardless of age, at the prospect of being so near to Her Majesty. Of course, their only other experience of the Royal Family would have been gained from watching the newsreels or seeing grainy photographs in the newspapers. Note the policemen in their white gloves. The officer on the left is putting a friendly, but firm hand on the jacket of the photographer beside him. Evidence of a more relaxed relationship between Press, Police and Royalty in the 1940s.

Below: The unmistakable interior of Huddersfield Town Hall. And the equally unmistakable profile of Sir Winston Churchill, the charismatic elder statesman credited with guiding Britain and the rest of the Free World through the dark days of the Second World War. The picture was taken in October 1951, a mere six years after the end of the war. Churchill looks distinctly frail in this photograph, but this is not surprising for he had already reached the age of 76. It is quite amazing, for those of us who remember Churchill as a world figure, to think that he was born in 1875, in a world that knew nothing of cars, aeroplanes, television, or even wireless! Churchill's visit to Huddersfield was made to support Lady Violet Bonham Carter's campaign to become elected as the Liberal MP for the Colne Valley constituency. On October 26th 1951, despite this apparent frailty Churchill was elected Prime Minister again, but the Conservative majority was very low. The youngest Conservative candidate in the 1951 election was 26 year-old Margaret Hilda Roberts, the ambitious young politician who went on to lead not only her party, but her country as Prime Minister. She later took her seat in the House of Lords and as Baroness Thatcher after one of the most dynamic political careers in British history.

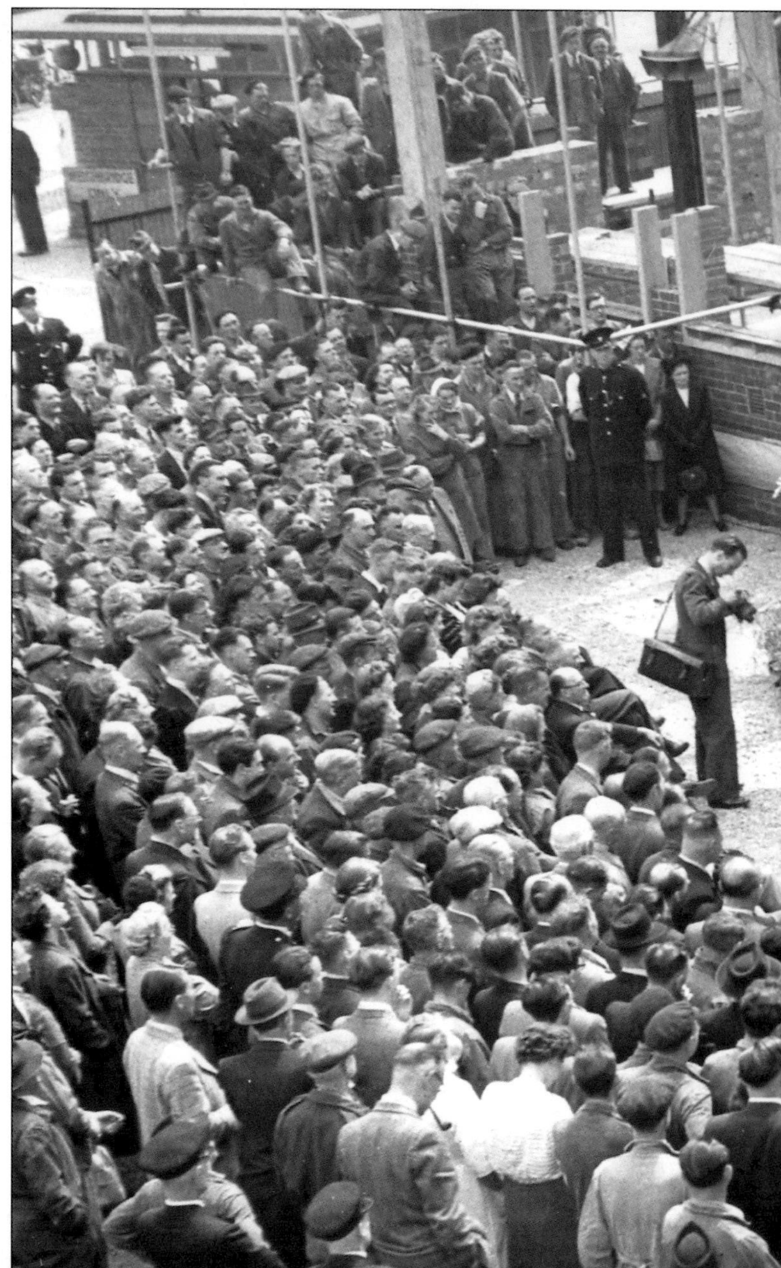

Above: This very formal affair was the laying of the foundation stone for the new office block at the I.C.I (Huddersfield) works. This part of the company has now been acquired by Zeneca. The manager of the I.C.I works at the time, Alderman G. B Jones, had another role in the town; when he was not overseeing the activities of the local branch of the world's most famous chemical company he was Mayor of Huddersfield. Alderman Jones is seen with his back to the camera in this picture, talking to Mr. George Wimpenny, representing the builders, J. Wimpenny & Sons of Linthwaite. The new office block represented a welcome investment in post war Huddersfield, coming as it did in June 1951, just six years after the end of the war.

R BARGAINS

The pictures on this page all relate to the visit of HRH Princess Margaret. The Princess had been invited to attend a special service at Huddersfield Parish Church conducted by the Rev. David Shepherd (who later went on to become the Bishop of Liverpool) who was the Curate of Church in April 1953 when these scenes were captured. Everyone looks rather cold on this chilly April day. Less than three months after these pictures were taken the crowds would turn out for parties on the streets of Huddersfield when the Queen was crowned Elizabeth II, in Westminster Abbey, on June 2nd. The scene along Byram Street is depicted when crowds of (mainly) women and children clammered to see Princess Margaret. Some of the little lads in the picture on the left look as if they are starting to get a bit fed up! The happy smiling faces elsewhere reflect the esteem in which the royal family was held at this time and the relatively low police presence demonstrates just how much times have changed since the 1950s in the area of royal security.

LONG LIVE THE QUEEN
Rushworths
Rushworths
Rushworths
MARSH
LINDLEY
OUTLANE
BIRKBY
FARTOWN
SHEEPRIDGE

Above: Her Majesty Queen Elizabeth II was crowned in a service at Westminster Abbey on June 2nd 1953. The event was celebrated throughout the country and beyond, and one spin-off from all the interest was that local churches and organisations held their own 'coronations' in which pretty young girls would be crowned 'queen' of the street, church or district. Here we see one such occasion, the crowning of the Coronation Queen at the Zion Wesleyan Chapel, Denby Dale. The *No Smoking* sign at the top-left of the picture would not be out of place these days, but in 1953 it would have been fairly unusual to see one in a public place. There are some lovely little faces in the group as they pose on the stage; the little girl in the centre of the front row seems to have had enough of the whole proceedings and the young lad towards the left has resorted to picking his nose! Most of the children in the picture will be at least 50 years of age at the time of writing. Where are they now, we wonder?

Left: Coronation decorations were displayed to a high standard at Rushworths department store in 1953. The whole town got behind the coronation celebrations that June, and no wonder, for this was one of the few occasions when the nation had had a mass celebration since the end of the war. The picture was taken looking towards John William Street of course, and Rushworth's had really gone to town with their decorations, with royal crests and even a portrait of the future Queen above the main entrance. This picture may well have been taken on a Sunday, judging by how sparse the streets appear, not to mention the fact that all the shops are closed. Overhead the power lines for the trolley buses can clearly be seen.

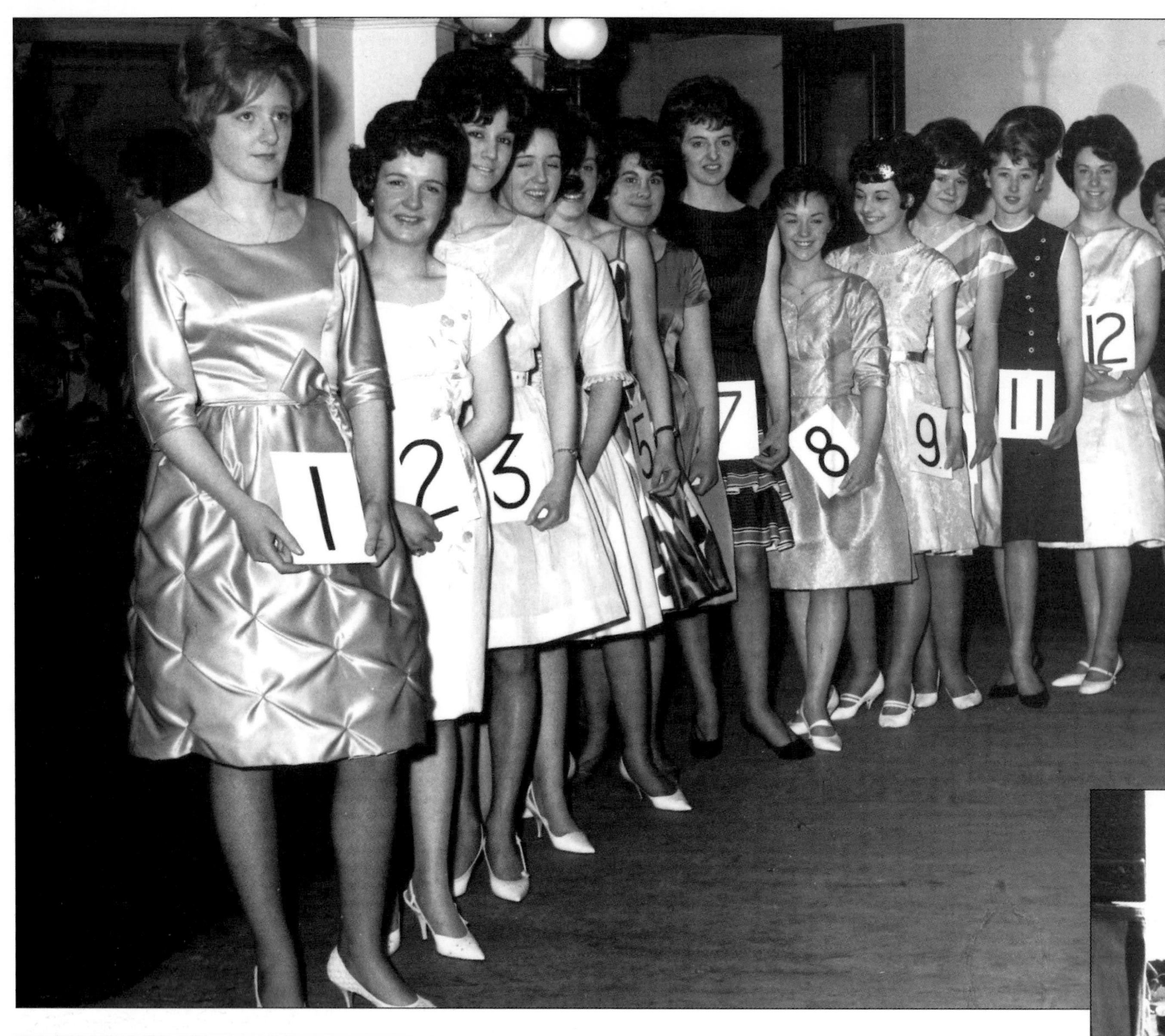
1
2
3
5
7
8
9
11
12

Left: Huddersfield Town Hall was the venue for this beauty contest. Seventeen lovely young ladies from the I.C.I works, each wearing a glamourous outfit either bought locally or (much more likely) made over several evenings at home especially for the contest. We do not know which of the delightful young ladies won the contest, but it could easily have been any of them, for they are all as pretty as a picture. These were the days before the idea of *political correctness* had been thought of, and none of the young ladies would have thought it demeaning to appear in a beauty contest in front of their workmates. And why should they!

Below left: Most carnivals were preceded by a procession, including floats and children in fancy dress; some of them, like this one, were fortunate enough to be led by a brass band. This photograph dates from 1953 and features the Hartshead and Liversedge carnival procession.

Below: Watching the Punch and Judy show was one of the most popular attractions for the children attending an annual gala. A good turnout was assured by the lovely sunny day for the Childrens' Gala Day of the local works of Huddersfield valve makers, Hopkinsons Ltd. The company is now part of the giant Wear group. This photograph is around 40 years old at the time of writing, dating, as it does, from 1959. It depicts an era considerably before our childrens' lives were so heavily influenced by television, indeed, this was the closest they got to peering at a 'square box' for hours on end!

Above: The re-opening of the refurbished Co-op in Huddersfield was a landmark in the development of the retailing organisation. This was November 1963 and who better to attend the event to perform the opening ceremony than the landlady of Coronation Street's Rovers Return - Annie Walker? Of course, the actress's real name was Doris Speed a beloved Coronation Street stalwart for many years. November 1963 was to become infamous, for this was when President Kennedy was assassinated. It was a tragic end to a year which had also seen the first woman (a Russian) in space, the Great Train Robbery and the commencement of the civil rights movement and subsequent unrest in America.

Right: When the ITV mast at Emley Moor came down in March 1969 the sections were spread over a wide area. In this photograph numbers can be seen on the debris. They had been added by the investigating engineers so that they could study the distribution of the wreckage after the pieces had been removed - in a bid to confirm the cause of the failure. The mast had a lift and a steel ladder running up inside it, evidence of which can be seen in this picture. Over a period of many weeks, a large team of workmen, three mobile cranes and several low-loaders were employed in the huge task of clearing the site. Fortunately nobody was injured in the catastrophic failure of the structure and damage was limited to the TV station base itself, a workmans' hut (which was crushed to matchwood and vacated only an hour before) and the end of Emley Moor Chapel.

480
520
450
450

Around the town centre

Above: This elevated view shows the buildings which surrounded the corner of High Street and Market Street as it appeared in 1957. The end of Macaulay Street can just be seen at the bottom right hand corner of the photograph and the Wire Works operated by Procter Bros. is shown facing the camera. Between Procter Bros. and the row of semi-derelict buildings there is a large advertising hoarding which looks rather modern (for 1957) and a little out of place. The product being promoted is Heinz Tomato Sauce, and the slogan upon it reads "You and Heinz together add that final tasty touch." In common with most towns in the process of redevelopment, Huddersfield found itself with large vacant areas in its centre awaiting new building works. These were often used as temporary car parking areas before the 'rise' of the multi-storey carparks which were to follow, as can be seen in the background of this scene.

Top left: The very orderly exterior of the Queen Hotel in Huddersfield's Market Street as it appeared in February 1953. The hotel was distinctive for the ornate ironwork balconies which added a touch of 'class' to the building. At the time of writing the structure remains and has found a new and useful contribution to the town as office accommodation. Towards the right of the picture, between two parked cars is the entrance to the Imperial Arcade. This part of the block had obviously been constructed as a warehouse, judging by the doors and gantry just to the right of the arcade entrance. This part of the block has been rebuilt as modern offices.

Bottom left: The Pack Horse Hotel in Kirkgate as pictured in August 1953. The establishment had changed little since the days when stage coaches called here on their way from Halifax to London. It remained a very popular hostelry until it was pulled down to make way for the Pack Horse shopping centre, the Kirkgate entrance to which being where the yard is to the right of the picture. In the same yard the 'Pack Horse Tap' can be seen. This was a popular 'watering hole' with a number of men in the town. Alongside the yard entrance is a notice board for Eddison Taylor and Booth, Estate Agents and Valuers in the town. Advertised here are houses for sale in Reinwood Road, one at Crosland Moor and another in Richmond Avenue, a mill at Rochdale, some manufacturing plant, an electric-driven crane and some antique and modern furnishings. Most people mourned the demise of this hotel; in the days when most local pubs were owned by the big brewers and there were few 'free houses' - and no such thing as guest beers, the Pack Horse offered a selection of beers that could not be purchased anywhere else in the town.

TETLEY
TOBACCO
TETLEY
WWU 370

SAVINGS BANK 1887
SAVINGS
THE SAVINGS BANK
Established
1818
THE SAVINGS BA
TRUSTEE SAVINGS BANK
Music & Records

Left: Market Street looked like this in May 1959. The picture was taken from the direction of Westgate, hence the ABC Cinema and Restaurant on the right of the picture. Kenneth Levell's shop which sold modern electrical appliances including fridges is on the left, and the Gledhill and Brook Time Recorder Company is the building facing the camera with the clock on the side of it. Next to Gledhill and Brook, at the top of Cloth Hall Street, is a white building housing the White Hart public house. At the time of writing the pub still enjoys a thriving trade from this location.

Below left: The corner of New Street (once known as Buxton Road) and Princess Street was the site of the large, black georgian building which housed *The Savings Bank.* The building was showing the effects of several decades' exposure to the smoke, soot and grime churned out by thousands of chimneys. The photograph was taken looking in the direction of Corporation Street, past the black 'Standard 10' motor car which is parked at the top of Princess Street. The very bold lettering on the masonry at the top of the bank building proclaims that it was established in 1887. A more modern, and modest sign above the New Street entrance suggests that the bank had already been taken over by the TSB by the time this view was recorded, in December 1964.

Below: An almost deserted scene at Folly Hall in Huddersfield. The route to the left at the traffic lights is St. Thomas's Road, leading to Longroyd Bridge. The premises on the corner housing Hinchliffe's butchers shop has now been pulled down, as has the mill behind it owned at the time by Joseph Lumb and Sons which is out of view in this picture. In modern times that site became the home for two night clubs and a bingo hall among other businesses here. On the right of the picture, the pub behind the traffic lights was the 'Yorkshire Hotel.' Since 1959, when this picture was taken, it has had a variety of uses, having had different names as night clubs. In the distance, and in the centre of the picture is Chapel Hill, with the Co-op and its clock tower peeping above the top of the buildings.

Right: Two-way traffic was permissible in October 1958 when this picture of Queen Street was taken. The photographer was looking in the direction of the Parish Church. Just out of shot, on the right of the scene, was the old Queen Street Mission which is now the Lawrence Batley Theatre. Much of the property on this street remains to this day but the shop fronts have been changed, in most cases, beyond recognition. Property on the left of the picture had to be pulled down in order to develop the new shopping centre when the old Market Hall was demolished. Some of the business names seen on the street will rekindle a memory or two for readers; Kneeshaw's the optician, Lauries Film Services, Clydesdale TV and Radio, Jay's and Buzby 'B' Stores to name just a few.

This picture dates from the end of the 1950s, a time which saw the birth of the CND movement and race riots on the streets of London. 1958 was also the year that saw the Munich air disaster, when 8 English footballers were among 21 passengers killed in an air crash in West Germany. Overseas the British army was involved in a serious escalation of violence in Cyprus. Five people were killed when British troops opened fire on hundreds of rioters on the streets of Nicosia.

Left: Overhead trolley bus lines dominate this picture which was taken in October 1958. The location is the junction of Northgate and Northumberland Street, popular with shoppers in the 1950s and the home of several small businesses which were very well supported at the time. Some of the traders who occupied the street and can be seen here include Kahn's Rainwear, D. Ramsdale the greengrocer, Hays the shoe shop, F & R Swallow the newsagents, Eastmans the butchers and Cockrofts the chemists. All the property on Northgate was pulled down to make way for the inner ring road. On the extreme left of the picture is the old Friendly and Trades Building. After remaining empty for many years it was stone-cleaned in the mid 1990s to prepare it for resale.

At the time this picture was taken the people of Huddersfield would have been interested in the major events happening on the world stage. In the USA manned space flight tests had been commissioned by the United States Government and the X15 manned rocket plane was due to be flown for the first time in 1959. The project was intended to test the effects of space travel on humans and pave the way for future missions. Nearer home Britain's Christopher Cockerell perfected his hover-craft device, the first in the world, which would later, after considerable devel-opment, form the basis of huge cross-Channel machines used by millions of travellers. Charles De Gaulle became Prime Minister of France during this year, the first time he had held an official government position since 1946.

Back on the home front, the death of one of England's most popular and successful composers, Ralph Vaughan Williams, was announced. He was aged 86.

Market Hall and the top of Cloth Hall Street are featured in this delightful picture from April 1959. More mature readers may remember that the area in the foreground was once covered by *rubber* setts. This was highly unusual. The innovative road surface was very hard wearing, but also very slippery when the weather was wet. On a rainy day you would seldom travel past this location without seeing someone fall over... or someone else just getting back up on their feet. By the time this photograph was taken the local authority had obviously decided that enough was enough, and

had resurfaced the road with conventional material. G.D Davies had the prime corner spot for their grocery business, and Crowther and Shaw's plumbers, electricians and refrigeration engineers operated their growing business next door. A fairly rare motorcar, and one which would be prized by collectors today, is the Rover 'Cyclops' parked outside G.D Davies' grocery store. The *Cyclops* took its name from the additional headlight mounted in the centre of the radiator grille.

Above: This shopping scene features the Country's best known retail store, Marks and Spencer, and several other smaller, national chains which were based on New Street. The picture dates from 1958 and was taken on a cold October day. To the right of Marks and Spencer is the entrance to Market Avenue, and next to that is *Etam.* True-Form and Stylo follow on before Dunn and Co. the Tailors is found on the left of the picture. The whole of this area is now pedestrianised. The road sign on the left of the picture is quite interesting. It is of a style no longer seen and describes how motors and horse drawn vehicles were banned from parking on shopping days between 10.00am and 4.00 pm - *except for the conveyance of goods to or from the premises in the road.* Of course, the modern shopping areas have built-in underground service access, so that heavy trucks making deliveries can do so 'behind the scenes' so as not to disrupt the flow of customers in the shop or the traffic on the high street.

If ever a vehicle symbolised 'nostalgia' it would surely be the Bedford light truck like the one pictured here. In the years after the war they were one of the most popular commercial vehicles on the road; virtually every medium to large scale business operated them at one time or another, and they always seemed a regular feature of post-war British films. This photograph shows one of the familiar vehicles making its way along New Street in January 1953. It is just passing the bus stop for Lockwood, having passed the premises of Woolworths, and the Pearl Assurance Company, Collinsons' Cafe, and Noels' Fashions. Other, smaller vehicles add character to the photograph on this crisp January afternoon.

The junction of High Street and New Street was the home of the Commercial Hotel, a Samuel Smith's house, and perhaps unusually in the same building as the public house, Hobson and Son the tobacconist. This was the busy junction where High Street, New Street, Buxton Road and Ramsden Street converged, and the young police officer on the right would have been on the look-out for any traffic violations which occurred at the crossroads. Looking down the street gives yet another view of the Burtons building, and on the left, the highly decorated dome of the Midland Bank. The photograph dates from the summer of 1950, a time when Britain was struggling to rebuild her economy after the long years of war. It is a sobering thought to remember that clothes rationing had ended only around a year before this picture was taken.

PRUDENTIAL
TO CAR
PARK
AYH485
485

MARKET
CAFE
STAFF VACANCIES

A tremendous record of how Huddersfield used to look in a view which will be sadly missed by everyone who knew the town in the 1950s. The photographer was looking down Cloth Hall Street, across New Street and in the direction of King Street when he took the picture. Perhaps the most sadly missed building in this view is the old Market Hall complete with highly distinctive clock tower. Equally distinctive were the Gothic-style turrets on the Market Hall roof. One wonders what the Market Hall would have looked like these days had it been preserved and cleaned up as is the case in some other neighbouring towns. The Burtons building with its white-facade is typically '1930s.' Virtually every town of any note had a Burtons outlet; the company enjoyed a period of major growth in the 1920s and 1930s and invested heavily in the distinctive buildings we see around the country today. It is interesting to see that many of the old Burtons buildings have been converted to hamburger restaurants as this new high street craze takes hold. This particular photograph dates from 1950.

HEYWOODS
HEYWOODS
HEYWOODS
CAFÉ
GIVE NYLONS
GIFTS
SLIPPERS
UNA 344

Left: It was Christmas time in 1958 when this picture was taken. Heywoods stood on the corner of Market Street and Threadneedle Street and was a popular and well-supported department store. The glowing fluorescent lights and bright shop windows contrast almost artistically with the darkness in this late winters' afternoon scene. Notices in the store window urge passers-by to 'give nylons this Christmas' along with slippers, umbrellas and cosmetics. Heywoods was well known for its cafe, always a popular meeting place and a welcome oasis for tired shoppers. In the late 1950s, when this scene was recorded, there were two such stores in Huddersfield, the other being Rushworth's in John William Street. Sadly, Heywoods was completely destroyed by fire in the early 1960s. The site is now occupied by various shops, a restaurant and offices.

Below: Buxton Road was the location for this nostalgic scene. The Co-op building would have been warm and inviting on this crisp winters' day; all the shoppers would have had the January sales firmly in mind as they browsed from store to store in this picture from 1961. The Co-op building on Buxton Road had dominated this spot since the end of the last century, though it was extended (see the right of the picture) with work being completed in 1936. There was a lot going on in the news when this picture was taken. The biggest story of the year was the Soviet Union's success in achieving the first manned space flight. It was also the year that the East Germans erected the Berlin Wall and, on the home front, George Blake was tried and convicted of spying for the Russians. He was sentenced to 42 years in gaol.

A lovely nostalgic scene from 1962 showing shoppers in the late afternoon going about their business, oblivious to the fact that they were being photographed for us to see almost 40 years later. The newspaper seller in the centre of the picture (by the underground gents' toilets) appears to be having a quiet spell, despite the billboard announcing a huge local garage blaze. The corner of Market Place was the location for the popular Freeman Hardy Willis shoe shop and John Sykes the firm of solicitors had the whole floor above. Several shoppers had taken refuge on the benches

in the the picture. These provided a welcome break in the warm sunshine from trailing around the shops. Barclays Bank can be seen on the right of the picture, and other familiar business names include Melias, Kendalls, The White House (the popular licensed restaurant),and George Garton and Son Ltd. Some delightful old motor vehicles complete the picture and add atmosphere to the scene. There is even a futuristic Citroen DS saloon at the traffic lights, quite rare at this time and destined to become an all-time classic vehicle.

WHITELEY'S Cafe
WHITELEY & SONS
CATERERS
HARRY SHARP & SONS
BROWNS
MMU 755
High Class Groceries and Provisions
Quality Fruit and Vegetables Fresh Daily

Whiteley's Cafe was practically an institution on Westgate, standing as it did next door to Harry Sharp and Sons, opposite The Plough Hotel. This photograph was taken in June 1950 and looks down towards another Huddersfield town-centre landmark, the Burtons building at the junction of John William Street and Market Place. It was obviously a warm, sunny afternoon, considering how virtually every shop has extended the white canvas shades above their windows. Notice how the overhead power lines for the trolley buses are tightly stretched, cobweb style along the street. The idea of them today seems almost ridiculous to the modern observer.

Above: The junction of Ramsden Street and Buxton Road as it looked in 1956. The photograph was taken on a cold October afternoon and depicts an area which is now pedestrianised. Buxton Road is now known as New Street. The building on the left of the picture, where two flag poles can just be seen, is the Town Hall. On the right of the picture the clock tower and dark outline of the Co-op can be seen. Overhead trolley wires complete the picture of the Huddersfield we knew around 40 years ago in a scene guaranteed to bring back memories for many.

Top: This scene was recorded in 1969 when the Hammerson shopping development on Buxton Road was new. The street has since been renamed New Street. The arcade shown here goes through to Albion Street and this photograph was taken from the top of Princess Street with the edge of the Co-op just showing on the left. This whole area, in common with many other parts of Huddersfield, has been completely pedestrianised in order to keep the cars and the shoppers a safe distance apart.

Below: Buxton Road, later to become New Street, looked like this is the mid-1950s. Many a tear was shed when the businesses featured here closed down, and the buildings which housed them were demolished in the late 1960s. The best-loved of the household names on the row was the Curzon Cinema. *The Curzon* was formerly the Picturedrome and many Huddersfield couples did their courting among the tightly-packed seats in the establishment. In this photograph the feature being shown was the Black Tent, starring Anthony Steel and a young Donald Sinden. The Curzon American snack bar did a healthy trade in coffee, coca cola and various tasty snacks. Henry Wigfall & Sons, the TV dealer was a branch of the national chain. The long established company had previously dealt in cycles and accessories before growing into the major high street electrical retailer we all know.

"FORMERLY THE PICTUREDROME, ...MANY HUDDERSFIELD COUPLES DID THEIR COURTING HERE"

Below: The junction of Cross Church Street and King Street on a quiet day in 1958. The corner site is obviously the prime retail spot and it was occupied by George Hutchinson the supplier of bankrupt stock, fancy goods and toys. Above Hutchinson's was Maison Terry - the ladies hairdresser, and above that were some offices occupied by the Co-operative Permanent Building Society. The Globe Hotel was adjacent to the Vacuum Repair Centre and Schofield & Co. Ltd., the paint and wallpaper specialist. Seeing the ladies hairdressers here reminds us of the way these services would be conducted in individual cubicles within the shop. The reason was that this element of privacy would ensure that only the hairdresser and her (or his) client would know whether the hair in question had been permed, coloured or treated in any other way. Ladies in days gone by were far more secretive and mysterious about their hairdressing arrangements.

Some may be surprised to learn that Huddersfield folk could enjoy a nice cup of tea and a sandwich while looking out over a relaxing view of Venice. To do this you had to either have a remarkable imagination or a 'window' seat at D'Agostino's ice cream parlour in the market! This picture was taken in 1960. Ice cream parlours, a craze with American connections, were less popular than the coffee bars which had sprung up in the 1950s, but D'Agostino's was popular with weary shoppers eager to find a clean comfortable resting place during busy bargain-hunting

D'Agostino
ICE CREAM PARLOUR

Right: It was all-change on the site which had formerly been occupied by the Theatre Royal when this photograph was taken in 1968. Many buildings, including offices used by the Local Authority, in this the locality were pulled down as a result of plans to redevelop the town centre. The substantial library building, which had been standing for less than 30 years when the picture was taken, remained intact despite the grand plans. In the background, on the left, the offices of Huddersfield's favourite newspaper *The Examiner,* can be seen. The work on the building site looks rather disorganised, with pieces of timber and reinforcing steel rods. We are sure the workmen knew exactly what they were doing, however, and the completed result stands comparison with any which can be seen in neighbouring towns.

Below: The Southgate Hotel was a popular public house with those interested in a traditional pub atmosphere and a quality pint served with a smile and a friendly word thrown in for good measure. Here it is overshadowed by the construction work in progress on the Telephone Exchange. The photograph dates from 1960, the dawn of the era which was to see tremendous development in Huddersfield.

At the flicks

Above: The chap with the startled look on his face is Berto Riselli, billed as 'the world's most powerful hypnotist with his amazing psychic hands.' According to the publicity he also had a first class *support*, but perhaps we shouldn't dwell on that. The photograph was taken in May 1951 and the theatre in question is the *Palace.* This was its heyday. Many of the country's best known stars have entertained from the stage of the Palace which over the years had been a very popular Music Hall. Sadly, with the dawn of the age of television and bingo audiences began to dwindle and it had to close down its theatrical activities. Towards the end, when attendances were very thin, one entertainer who could still 'pack 'em in' was Frank Randle. He was well known for beginning his act by walking on stage, giving an almighty burp, and proclaiming "Ee A'v had some ale toneet!!!" the Palace saw service as a bingo hall for many years but, at the time of writing, has ceased this activity too.

Above: This picture dates from the mid 1950s and features the ornate facade of the Grand Cinema, Huddersfield. The building was located at the beginning of Manchester Road near its junction with Chapel Hill and the cinema was part of the ABC group. Always considered to be the 'poor relation' to its sister cinema, the Ritz it eventually stopped showing feature films and afterwards remained empty for a number of years. In recent years (relative to the time of writing) the building was taken over by Comet, the electrical retailers, who have kept the beautiful facade by putting the modern entrance and car park at the rear.

Left and below: The 1930s canvas-top saloon car could be deceptive to anyone attempting to put a date on this picture. The photograph was, in fact, taken in July 1953 and it shows the unusual tall Georgian style walls of the Tudor Cinema and Cafe. The exterior of the building is remembered for its ornate glass and iron work canopy, along with the fact that the roof had the name 'Hippodrome' painted on it long after it had been changed to 'Tudor.' Many aerial photographs of Huddersfield, including at least one featured in this book, show the cinema roof which had become something of a landmark. As a cinema the establishment was unusual in that it had retained the theatre-style seating arrangements complete with 'gods' and a side balcony in the circle which combined to afford a very unsatisfactory view of the flat cinema screen.

Right: All the atmosphere of a wet November evening in Huddersfield is captured in this photograph from the mid 1950s. Market Street was the location of the shot, the ABC Ritz the dominant feature of the scene. The photograph has an almost artistic air about it, though this was not the intention when it was taken. Cinema-goers could enjoy the delights of the *Reluctant Debutante* starring Rex Harrison and Kay Kendall, or the *Underwater Warrior* at the time this picture was taken. Both carried a 'U' certificate. This venue was one of the larger ones of its type, offering, as it did a 2000 seating capacity. The Ritz also offered civilised dining in its own restaurant. The popularity of the cinema industry has seen its ups and downs during the period between 1950s and the present day. Film makers were insulated from the worst depths of the problem as they have been able to sell their products to the television companies. Thankfully cinema is now enjoying the return of its former levels of popularity.

"IN THE 1950S THERE WERE OVER TWO DOZEN CINEMAS IN HUDDERSFIELD"

Left: Children of employees of the Huddersfield I.C.I works would look forward to the annual childrens' treat organised by the firm. This photograph records some of the party-goers leaving the Ritz Cinema after the event which was held in 1955. The youngsters certainly look very smart, and one or two of them can be seen opening their presents as they leave the cinema. Some of the forthcoming attractions at the cinema are advertised on the front of the building, including 'The Raid' and another feature film starring Kirk Douglas, which seems to have caught the attention of one of the ladies in the foreground.

Above: It was *Carry On Up The Khyber* at the ABC Cinema, Market Street, in March 1969. The ABC was, of course, formerly *The Ritz*, and many Huddersfield folk were devastated when it was announced that this fine old building (completed just before the outbreak of the Second World War) was to be pulled down to make way for a Sainsburys supermarket and other shops. In addition to the normal cinema facilities it had a full theatre stage with dressing rooms and associated internal services. The Huddersfield Operatic Society and the Huddersfield Light Opera Company both used the stage for their annual productions. It also had a Wurlitzer organ, a restaurant and, before the alterations were made to convert it into two cinemas, a seating capacity of two thousand.

Below: *Holmfirth Laundry* and the *Radio Craft* shop on Albion Street got in on the act when the photographer recorded this scene outside the ABC Ritz. It is interesting to notice the telephone number on the shiny Volkswagen van - 'Holmfirth 44' - an indication of the age of the picture and the low levels of telephone ownership at the time. This was the Ritz in pre-facelift days, before the bright new electrically-lit fascia. John Wayne was starring in *The High and Mighty* with Claire Trevor, Robert stack and others. It enjoyed the benefit of *Cinemascope* of course, along with the lesser-known advantage of *Warnercolor*, according to the bill board. The Ritz was owned by Associated British Cinemas (ABC) and was the venue for many live performances by the great and the good - including The Beatles and Sir Cliff Richard.

Sporting life

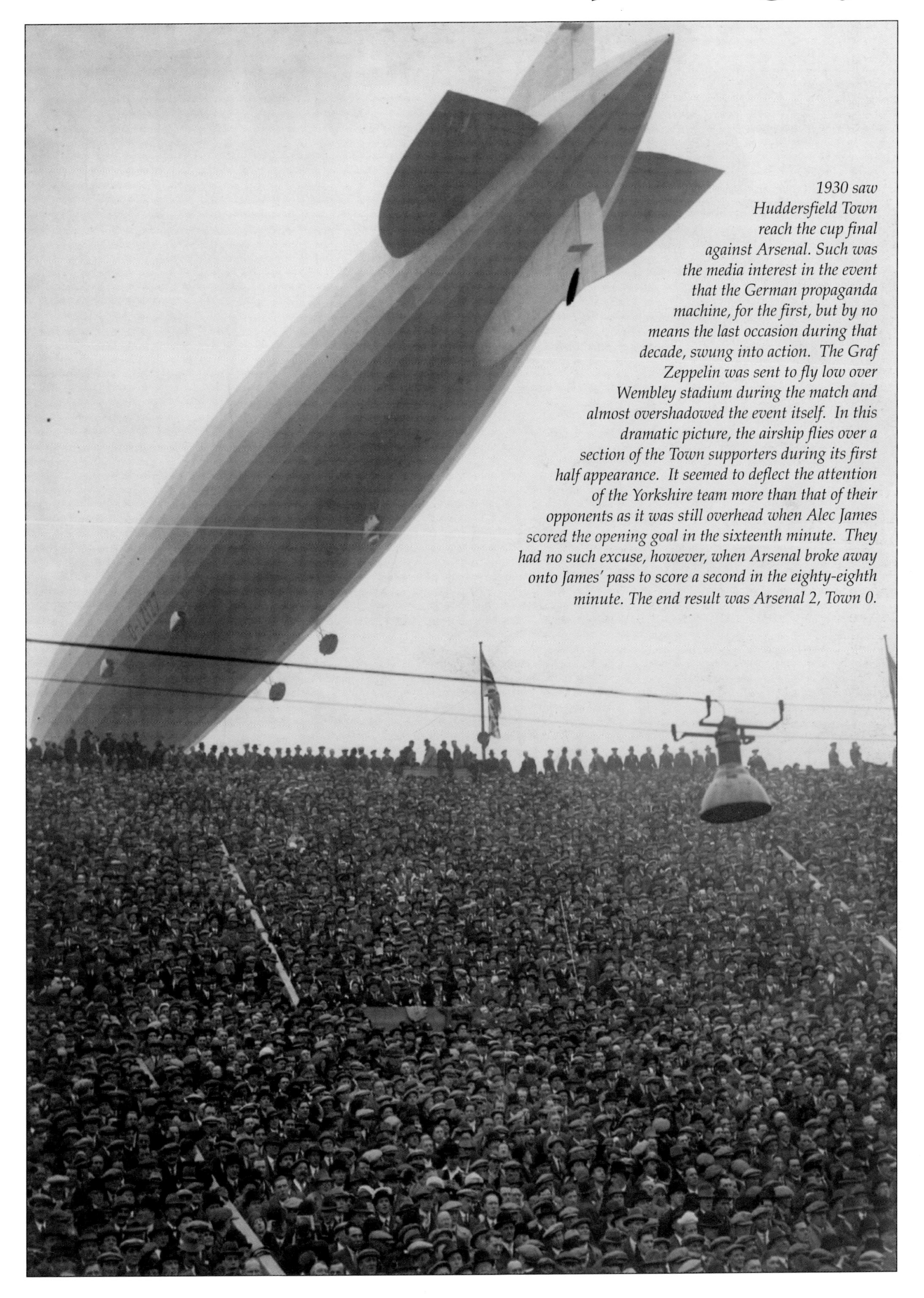

1930 saw Huddersfield Town reach the cup final against Arsenal. Such was the media interest in the event that the German propaganda machine, for the first, but by no means the last occasion during that decade, swung into action. The Graf Zeppelin was sent to fly low over Wembley stadium during the match and almost overshadowed the event itself. In this dramatic picture, the airship flies over a section of the Town supporters during its first half appearance. It seemed to deflect the attention of the Yorkshire team more than that of their opponents as it was still overhead when Alec James scored the opening goal in the sixteenth minute. They had no such excuse, however, when Arsenal broke away onto James' pass to score a second in the eighty-eighth minute. The end result was Arsenal 2, Town 0.

In the aftermath of the Wembley tragedy and disappointment, there was little to console the side as they arrived home on the Monday tea-time. Results elsewhere that weekend had plunged the Club further into the relegation mire and it needed full points from the remaining two games to have a chance of escaping the drop. After tea at the Town Hall, they travelled to Leeds Road and in a display of great character Stoke City were beaten 3-0. On the following Saturday, Manchester City were the visitors and a place in division one was the prize for the victors. A single goal - scrambled over the line by Barclay half way through the second period - was sufficient to see Town through and City relegated. At the end there were contrasting scenes of relief, joy and despair amongst the 35,100 spectators.

Below: The football league proper re-started after a seven year break in August 1946. Town struggled at the wrong end of the table until the arrival of Doherty at Christmas, after which it became increasingly frustrating for players and supporters due to terrible weather conditions. During this time the management decided to take the team to Holland and Scotland to seek friendly fixtures. With 5 ft drifts of snow on the terraces, Leeds Road was unplayable from the end of January until mid March. Even when the thaw eventually arrived, it left a legacy of atrocious playing conditions.

The photograph was taken at the Valley, Charlton on 8th March 1947, a match of great significance to Town's efforts to avoid relegation. Thompson, Bateman and Doherty scored for Town without reply. The attendance was 27,805.

At the end of the sixties Huddersfield Town's new-found status required some upgrading of the Leeds Road ground. The main stand seating was extended over the 'Paddock' area terracing during the summer of 1970. An additional 2,000 seats increased the seating capacity to 6,400, all accommodated in this west stand. This, together with extended office accommodation, improved catering facilities, plus the construction of a new television gantry gave the stadium an appearance which remain unchanged until its demolition in 1994.

Wheels of time

Above: A little girl and her dad examine a cut-away display of a Morris commercial vehicle at the opening of C.H. Mitchell's new showrooms. We could just make out that the price on the bonnet (presumably for a vehicle which is not cut away!) is £747. It was fairly typical for businesses in the 1950s to purchase a running chassis from a dealer and fit a vehicle body suitable for their particular needs separately.

Left: The Trinity Garage Co. Ltd. was a well known supplier of Rootes Group cars. This photograph shows their new premises in April 1953. They were located on Northgate and the company also had a dealership in neighbouring Halifax. This interior view of the showroom shows three Hillman Minx models on display as part of a promotion for the popular Hillman saloon.

Behind the scenes at C. H Mitchell's Morris dealership in the mid 1950s. The white-coated foreman offers advice on a problem with this Morris saloon and there is evidence of mechanical and body repairs in progress. The workshop looks very well organised with its innovative easy-access pits, overhead engine hoists and modern four post vehicle lift in the far corner. It also looks huge - there are well over 20 vehicles in the process of being repaired here, and almost as many mechanics in the scene. It must have been a hefty commercial organisation in terms of the local motoring scene at the time. The condition of the roads and the more primitive nature of the vehicles concerned meant that cars and trucks would spend considerably more hours in the workshop for every thousand miles they travelled.

Top right: Several fine vehicles seen at the opening of C.H. Mitchell's new premises in Southgate. This shot shows two fine Riley saloons awaiting delivery to their proud new owners. Stylish and fast, they were every schoolboys' dream in the mid 1950s; they epitomised the joys of family motoring for the lucky ones who could afford it, with their wood and leather interiors, running boards and sweeping wings.

Middle right: Saloons and commercial vehicles displayed together at the premises of Trinity Garage in Northgate, Huddersfield. The Sunbeam Talbot, on the left, is dwarfed by the large Humber saloon, and both vehicles look very stylish in comparison to the rather glum-looking 'commercials' behind them. Price comparisons are interesting too; the Humber saloon was offered at £725 in 1953, whilst the Commer 25 cwt *super capacity* van could be yours for £650. All vehicles were subject to purchase tax which added 17 1/2 % to the price. On the left of the picture the chassis-cab with the nervous expression on its 'face' is a Karrier Bantam, complete with starting

handle and on sale for £635. The advertising poster on the left proclaims the recent success enjoyed by the Sunbeam company in the International Alpine Trial of 1952. Sunbeam Talbot's were accomplished rally contenders in the 1950s.

Bottom right: An elevated view of the Trinity Garage showroom in Northgate. On the right is a display of 'modern' electric petrol pumps. The raised circular display on the right of the picture offers various car accessories including car clocks, not something you could count on having in your new model in 1953.

MG
MORRIS SIX
2215 C.C.

Above: It was party time at the opening of C.H. Mitchell's new motor showroom when this photograph was taken in July 1953. The successful Morris dealership had relocated from their old premises in East Parade to this new, purpose-built showroom in Southgate, Huddersfield. The group of people seen in this picture are standing in front of a Morris van which is about to be delivered to the town's favourite *pop* producer, Ben Shaws. It certainly looks attractive in its sparkling new paintwork. In the days before the big retail motor groups were established the dealerships in Huddersfield were controlled by long established private firms. The following names are certain to bring back memories: Brockholes Motor Company (Ford), W.H. Atkinson (Austin), C.H. Mitchell (Morris), Rootes Group (Hillman, Humber, Sunbeam Talbot, Commer, Karrier etc.) - Trinity Garage Company. Virtually all the new foreign cars sold in the area at the time were supplied by Newtons of Viaduct Street.

Left: The opening of C. H. Mitchell's new Morris showroom was a proud occasion for the company. It was only now, in the early 1950s, that the motor trade really began to take off. These two gentlemen can be seen examining a cut-away display model of a Morris Six engine. Boasting a capacity of 2215 c.c the engine was noted for its smoothness and pulling power. It found its way into many Morris saloons and light commercial vehicles over the years. In the corner of the showroom was another display featuring the first vehicle produced by Morris Commercial Cars Ltd., in 1924. On the wall there hangs a portrait picture of H.M. Queen Elizabeth, no doubt positioned there to mark her recent coronation.

Right: Some very expensive machinery receiving the first-class attention it deserves and requires to keep it in tip-top condition, at Appleyards of Huddersfield. The photograph was taken towards the end of 1971. Note the vintage Rolls Royce in the far corner of the workshop, registration number CC 4908, a fine example of the marque undergoing engine repairs. It was once said, though the statement is difficult to verify, that at the early part of the century there were more Rolls Royces in Huddersfield than there were in London. Certainly, Huddersfield had one of the most successful main dealers in the country - Rippon Brothers. That firm had disappeared by the time that Appleyards were carrying on their Rolls Royce - related activities in the town as depicted by this photograph.

Below: The crowded showroom display at C.H. Mitchell's in this further view of their opening promotion, when the level of trade in Morris and allied vehicles warranted the creation of new display premises. It may seem unusual to modern vehicle buyers to see the mixture of commercial and private motor transport on view in the same showroom, but this was often the way motor dealers would operate in times past.

"...IT WAS ONCE SAID THAT THERE WERE MORE ROLLS ROYCES IN HUDDERSFIELD THAN THERE WERE IN LONDON..."

Long summers

Above: The 1950s saw the growth in popularity of coach trips. These would be organised by small independent operators, or would be regular events run by Church groups, youth clubs or other local societies. As the 1950s progressed, travel by coach began to threaten the supremacy of railway-based excursions in terms of popularity. We are not sure what the destination was for this smart party of trippers, but they look well equipped for a day out in the sun. Coaches like this one all seemed to have a lot more character than their modern equivalents; you can almost smell the distinctive aroma of the wood, fabric and tobacco on the vehicle as you look at this picture. The sound of the engine and transmission had a character all of its own too. The whining axle and crunching gearbox would punctuate the journey to the seaside... but nobody would care much, as long as the weather held!

Below: Rawthorpe Childrens' Field Day attracted huge crowds of all different ages when it took place in June 1953. Most of the children seen in the picture would have been born after the end of the war, but they would have been used to difficult times, shortages and 'making do' during their short lives. At the time of writing most of these delightful youngsters will be in the 50s, with children and grandchildren of their own.

Above: Primrose Hill Gala Day from a photograph taken in the mid 1950s. All the children seem to be turned out very smartly, 'Sunday-best' being the order of the day. Looking at the photograph brings it home to us just how much childrens' fashions have changed in the space of almost half a century; the girls don't look *too* dissimilar to the appearance of modern girls on their way to a party, but the boys look entirely different. Just try making your little lad wear short trousers, a tank top and a blazer... let alone a tie!

Top right: The caption on this picture could easily be 'Fishing for Trouble.' The concentration reflected on the faces of the little-ones is intense as they watch their friends dip their fishing rods into the tin bath. The scene was recorded at Hartshead and Liversedge Carnival in 1953. The tin bath would have been a routine part of family life for most of these youngsters. Inside toilets and bathrooms were not a feature of every house at this time - and the Friday night bath in front of the fire was a memorable part of many folks' lives. It was obviously much easier to entertain children in the '50s; the expense involved with keeping modern kids happy, with everything from hamburgers to computers, seems to be taken for granted by them these days!

Below right: This photograph was taken just a week after the Coronation of Her Majesty Queen Elizabeth II in June 1953. Parents and their little-ones are seen enjoying a warm sunny afternoon at Linthwaite Carnival. At this time virtually every small town and village had a well-attended carnival each year. It was a chance to get together as a community, entertain the children and raise money for local good causes. 1953 was a busy year in terms of news events, quite apart from the British coronation. It was the year that Soviet tyrant Stalin died, attracting six mile queues of mourners eager to confirm that he had, in fact, passed on. It was also the year that J.F Kennedy married Jacqueline Lee Bouvier, the society photographer.

Top left: The fancy-dress competition winners pose for a picture beside the refreshment caravan at the Hartshead and Liversedge Carnival. The caravan would have been a popular stopping off point as people made their way around the carnival site. Tea, cakes and snacks would have been on offer to the hungry masses from the cute little caravan on the corner of the site. The picture dates from the mid-1950s and manages to capture the mood of the event very well indeed.

Above: You made your entertainment in *those* days. This group of youngsters started early, they were contestants in a Fancy Dress competition at Rawthorpe Childrens' Field Day in 1953. Prizes were on offer for the best outfits, but it was taking part that counted more than the accolade of 'coming first.' The boy in the centre of the picture wears a sign on his hat to let us know he is 'canned up.' Mother Hubbard and a hospital patient were other excellent entries, clearly a lot of thought and effort had gone into their outfits.

Middle left: The excitement grew on the faces of the dozen-or-so children pictured here, all aboard the Lindley Carnival and Gala Day Express. The expressions on the faces of the watching parents makes an interesting record too; several of them appear to have their minds on other things! The youngsters all look very smart and well wrapped-up. The photograph was taken in June 1953, the same month as the coronation of HRH Queen Elizabeth II. No doubt that occasion caused its fair share of excitement for these little ones too.

Below left: A crowd of onlookers seen at the Longley and Lofthouses Carnival. It was 1953, a year which saw the Coronation of Queen Elizabeth II, the climbing of Everest by Sir Edmund Hillary of New Zealand and Sherpa Tenzing of Nepal. It was also the year that the revolutionary but ill-fated *Comet* airliner took to the skies, and the war in Vietnam, which shook the world, broke out. Thoughts about most of these world affairs would be far away from the minds of these Huddersfield people when they turned out to enjoy their local carnival.

Above: Pony rides were a popular attraction at the Summer Entertainments in Greenhead Park. The children here are obviously quite confident about their short journey on horseback, certainly the ponies look placid enough. July and August each year would see a whole range of activities designed to keep children, as well as adults entertained. Every year the organisers would attempt to make the attractions even better. They certainly drew the crowds and happy days out at the 'entertainments' at Greenhead Park are fondly remembered by thousands of Huddersfield folk to this day.

Right: Another example of the organised entertainment laid on for the *Summer Entertainment* programme. The paddling pool was out of bounds to youngsters for a couple of hours while various elderly model enthusiasts, dressed in waders, demonstrated the art of sailing model boats. We have to remember that these were the days before Noel Edmonds and *Nintendo* computer games - so almost *any* opportunity for a bit of entertainment was grasped eagerly! The picture dates from the mid 1950s. Of course, it would have been every little lads' dream to own one of the intricately-detailed model boats in the photograph. Several of their dads would have had many stories to tell them about life at sea from experience gained only a few years earlier in the war. Despite the end of the Second World War in the previous decade, peace was elusive throughout the 1950s.

The main concern for ordinary British citizens was the effect of hostilities in Suez and Korea, and the danger of being drawn into the French war in Vietnam. There was the ever-present threat of the new atomic age as the East squared-up to the West in a *cold war* which was to last several decades. It was a time when many overseas colonies were challenging Britain and other major powers in their quest for independence. This would later change the nature of the undeveloped world in the 1960s.

Above: On a hot summers day the paddling pool at Greenhead Park was a huge attraction for kiddies as this picture shows. Unfortunately the pool was drained for health reasons, along with most other similar facilities, and is no longer in use. The picture was taken in 1955, the same year that Disneyland opened in Los Angeles, but it would be quite some time before the children of Huddersfield would be crossing the Atlantic to enjoy their summer holidays abroad.

Below: The delightful, tree-lined main avenue in Greenhead Park was a favourite location for Huddersfield folk looking for somewhere to relax and take it easy in the warm summer sunshine.
The photograph was taken in 1954, less than 10 years after the end of the Second World War, and people would at last be getting their lives in order after the disruption caused by the conflict.

Above: Another attraction at the Summer Entertainments in Greenhead Park was the miniature railway ride. Here a beautifully detailed locomotive prepares to take eleven youngsters on a short journey in the park, the thrill of the prospect is clearly visible in their faces as their parents look on. The ride was obviously very popular, judging by the long queue of eager participants behind the fence. The photograph dates from the early 1950s.

Left: The Open-Air Theatre was the venue for a talent spotting contest in Greenhead Park in the mid 1950s. This audience looks as if it would be quite difficult to please, judging by the serious looks on the faces of some of the people here. Generally though, people remember the talent-spotting events with fond memories of the sympathetic reception given to most would-be performers. Looking at this scene it is clear that the talent-spotting contest was very popular with local people but it is difficult to imagine how the people in the background would have seen and heard what was going on!

June 1962 at the Leeds Road Sports Ground owned by I.C.I. The occasion was the Childrens' Gala and this photograph was taken to record the entrants in the fancy dress competition. The children all look lovely, their parents had taken a lot of trouble to make these imaginative costumes from a variety of household items. Our favourite is the little girl seen fourth from the left in the costume made from old newspapers with the clever title 'Miss Print.' It must have been a difficult job for the judges picking a worthy winner from this selection.

Outskirts

May 1951, though the clarity of this picture belies the fact that it is almost half a century old. The location is, of course, Kirkburton, the picturesque Pennine village on the outskirts of Huddersfield which has retained most of its character and charm despite the ravages of time. The tiny white notice in the window of the Midland Bank indicates that trading hours at this branch were on Wednesday and Friday only. But at least they had a branch in the days before telephone banking and the reduction of the number of branches of all banks became fashionable. The atmosphere of the village really comes across in the picture with the petrol filling station, the old mill in the background and the small cottages in the alleyway.

1951 was the year that Winston Churchill again became Prime Minister and the Festival of Britain on the South Bank of the Thames temporarily lifted the post-war gloom in Britain. The Festival was opened by the King and Queen and attracted thousands of visitors from all over the country - including many from Huddersfield.

A rare photograph from February 1964. Members of the Colne Valley Hunt assemble at the Nags Head Inn at Ainley Top. The master of the hounds was struggling to control the twenty excited dogs who were eager to set off on the hunt. Some very well-heeled supporters look on as the preparations get underway, and one or two of them seem bemused at the prospect of having their photograph taken. No sign of protesters at the hunt of course, for that is a more recent phenomenon. Many other aspects of British life were different too; 1964 saw the appointment of the first coloured policeman (in Gloucestershire) and the average manual workers' wage reach just short of £17 per week. Two months after this scene was recorded television viewers would have their options extended with the launch of the long-awaited BBC 2 service. It was the era of the *swinging sixties,* a time which would change our ideas and attitudes forever.

"TWENTY EXCITED DOGS WERE EAGER TO SET OFF ON THE HUNT"

Penistone Road, Fenay Bridge as it appeared in 1954 is featured in this highly nostalgic scene. The photographer was looking in the direction of Huddersfield when he took the picture. To a large extent the scene has changed little right up to this day. The picture is a product of the work of Morris Bray, perhaps Huddersfield's best known commercial photographer; it really captures the mood of the mid 1950s. The lovely old motor cars are the only real clue as to the age of the picture - you can almost hear the whining axles and smell the leather upholstery as you gaze at them here.

Top right: North Road, Kirkburton is featured in this photograph. It dates from August 1952 and shows the street which was virtually unchanged in appearance since well before the beginning of the Second War. The motorcar approaching the camera (a small Morris dating from the 1930s) is being driven by an elderly gentleman. We trust the photographer leapt out of its path in time. Turnshaw Lane can be seen going to the left in the middle-distance and the church clock on the tower in the distance indicates that the picture was taken in the late afternoon. Interestingly, Belisha Beacons can be seen on the crossing in the foreground. They take their name from the Minister of Transport at the time of the 1930 Road Traffic Act, Mr. Hore-Belisha.

Below right: A delightfully nostalgic scene recorded in 1952. Residents of Kirkburton will recognise their village, though there have been changes to the scene since the picture was taken. Perhaps the most obvious is the covering of the cobbled road surface with a layer of tarmac and the road is, now, of course, much busier than it appears here. Still, North Road retains much of the charm that is characterised

here as we look at it almost 50 years later. We can't help wondering what has become of the two ladies and three children pictured nearest the camera; even the children would be in their 50s by now. Do they remember pushing their little baby brother or sister up the hill with their mum? We may never know.

Bird's eye view

An elevated view of Lindley, taken from an aeroplane at an altitude of 1000 ft in September 1974. The long, straight road running from half way up the right hand side of the picture to the top left is, of course, Acre Street. In the top left hand corner is the unmistakable tall white structure we recognise as Lindley Clock Tower. Half way up the right hand side of the picture the half-empty Infirmary car park is featured.

A marvellous photograph showing the changing face of Huddersfield in the mid 1960s. The recently-built Fire Station can be seen towards the top of the picture, near the Upper Head Row Bus Station. Buildings on the north side of Buxton Road were in the process of being cleared from this scene in order to create the site for the new C & A department store and Buxton House. The picture affords a good view of the 'new' Police Station and Magistrates Courts situated in front of the bus station. The Curzon Cinema is just visible at the bottom of the photograph. Sadly it was pulled down less than two years after this scene was recorded. Huddersfield's original development plan was drawn up in 1954 to be approved by the Minister of Local Government and Housing. This was no foregone conclusion, for in the post-war resource-starved economy there were strict controls on what kind of local authority development could be undertaken. The plan was reviewed, updated and approved in 1968, and a further round of redevelopment was set in motion on 13.5 acres of the town centre. Huddersfield, in common with many other similar towns of her size, was eager to attract people from the surrounding area into her shopping and entertainment centres. The schemes met with some success, for by 1983 Huddersfield was the third largest shopping area in the whole of the West Riding. Milestones along the way included new stores built by major retailers, such as Hillards (1979) and Sainsburys (1982).

An aerial view of the very heart of Huddersfield as it was going through the changes which gave us the retail shopping centre we know today. The Corporation was in an almost unique position when it came to the redevelopment of the centre because it owned much of the land and property in question. In 1920, through a special Act of Parliament, and at a cost of £1,300,000 the Corporation acquired the Freehold of 4,300 acres, including the entire central part of the town. Initially the acquisition was managed by the Estates Department of the Corporation until 1953 when the title was altered to the Estates and Property Management Department, with the additional function of managing and maintaining all Corporation-owned properties. The development of the centre of Huddersfield was a massive undertaking on the part of the Local Authority. A report submitted by them in the 1960s gave an indication of the way they were thinking. It said that "Huddersfield's buildings of architectural value and quality are irreplaceable; their retention will strengthen the sense of continuity between the past and the present." Thankfully the planners of the day recognised the value of Huddersfield's wide streets and distinctive late Victorian architecture which gives the town a 'feeling of substance' which characterises the finest towns in the West Riding. Most of these were left intact. St. George's Square and the the truly magnificent facade of the railway station are, along with Queen Street, outstanding jewels in the crown of the central area.

The railway had arrived in Huddersfield in 1847 - the foundation stone of which was laid by Earl Fitzwilliam in 1846. The ceremony was attended by thousands of local folk who enjoyed a special public holiday for the day, accompanied by a Civic Procession and the ringing of bells throughout the Borough. The station facade is often referred to as one as the finest in Britain.

HIPPODROME

Many old landmarks can be seen in this aerial view from 1965. The roof of the Hippodrome can be seen just right of centre and the much-loved, and now lost, Market Hall is featured just above it. On Ramsden Street the old Police Station and Local Government Offices stand on the site which would later become the location of the new Market Hall, less than 10 years after this scene was captured. It was to replace the old market hall which closed its doors for the last time at the end of March 1970.
Construction work can be seen underway on the buildings which would become part of Huddersfield Polytechnic - later *Huddersfield University* of course - a seat of learning with a national reputation capable of attracting students from all parts of the country.
The bottom left of the picture includes a rooftop view of the Co-op building. This much-photographed retail emporium was designed in 1893 by J.Berry Esq. but it was not opened as a store until 1906. The local co-operative movement began in Meltham in the early years of the nineteenth century. There were a few false starts with the movement and eventually the Huddersfield Industrial Society was established in 1860, the forerunner of the Co-op we know and love today.
The pedestrianisation of New Street was to take place in the mid-1970s. The reasoning behind it was faultless; most shopping activities take place on foot and it makes sense to keep pedestrians away from the noise, smell and dangers associated with motorcars. Two car parks (Alfred Street and the Civic Centre) would allow motorists to park and then walk to the shopping areas, though planners always recognise that most people will not walk far! All the shops facing New Street had rear access and so the argument for pedestrianising the area was compelling. In doing so the planners wanted to create a safe, sheltered, wide shopping area - assisted by the thoughtful deployment of trees, seating and lighting. The result of the efforts of the planners is enjoyed by shoppers today.

A view from the south east of Huddersfield town centre which records the layout of the town in the mid 1960s. The Shore Head roundabout is seen on the left of the picture. Towards the top of the photograph, in the centre, the old Market Hall complete with distinctive ridged roof is apparent, and behind the market some of the new buildings which heralded the start of the modern age of shopping in the town are already in place. Keen eyes may just be able to make out the lettering on the roof of the Hippodrome Theatre in the centre-left of the view. After a spell as the 'Tudor Cinema' from 1930 it became the Essoldo some years later, finally ending its days when a devastating fire resulted in demolition in 1967. In this view there is still much evidence of a large amount of town centre domestic housing. In common with many, if not most northern towns there was a drive to build housing estates outside the centre in the 1920s and '30s. This was made possible by the growing network of public transport which allowed people to live some distance away from their place of work. Many of the housing estates were built on the exposed hill-sides away from the industrialised Colne Valley. Some of these estates were located at Fartown, Sheepridge, Dalton, Birchencliffe and Newsome. Under a slum clearance plan older districts in the town were cleared. Following the end of the Second World War there was a drive to improve the quality of housing as well as the quantity. It is easy to forget that inside lavatories and bathrooms were not universally enjoyed by local people and it was not until the late 1960s that these facilities could *almost* be taken for granted.

At work

May 1951 saw the new television station at Holme Moss nearing completion. This photograph shows a variety of contractors' cars and vans which add a nostalgic flavour to the scene; the early Landrover and Ford Populars look particularly appropriate to the period. The station buildings would have been considered very modern in architectural terms, quite in keeping with the new age of television that they were meant to serve. Another interesting point illustrated by this picture, is that the base of the mast itself was supported by a two-inch diameter ball bearing. This design detail allowed the mast to move a few fractions of a degree between the supporting cables when the wind was very strong. The road over to Woodhead can just be seen to the right of the picture.

A supply of fresh bread is delivered to Home Moss T.V Station by the BBC bus driver, Mr. H. Armitage. The scene dates from 1954 and the BBC mini-bus was the only means of transport for supplies, mail and personnel to the station. Of course, one or two members of staff had their own transport, but the majority would rely on the staff driver, Mr. Armitage, who was used to battling through all but the most difficult weather conditions to keep the station stocked up and operating.

Rather them than us... these riggers are about to climb the Holme Moss Television Mast as the station nears completion. The date was May 1951; this activity was taking place at the very dawn of the television age.

A small team of workmen and volunteers battle against the odds to clear a way through the snow. The route leads to the Holme Moss Television Station and this was not the first or last time that it had been cut off by deep falls of snow. The staff at Holme Moss were accustomed to the weather and the threat of being isolated in the winter months. Because of this they carried supplies of food and blankets to see them through any temporary cut-off periods. This photograph dates from January 1952.

Below: Another scene from the open-day at Hanson Haulage's new depot on Leeds Road. The large industrial unit would soon be crammed with various loads destined for all parts of the Country. In this picture we see four or five luton-bodied Bedford trucks lined up against the loading platform beneath signs (just visible on the right hand edge of the picture) indicating the destination of the trucks concerned. Right at the back of the warehouse area, towards the left, a small fork-lift truck is parked. Generally speaking the loading and unloading of trucks was a rather labour-intensive operation, with speed and accuracy being the key to success and keeping the customer happy.

Bottom: Arriving in town in your personal helicopter in 1962 must have been the equivalent of popping across to France on board the QEII to buy a French loaf. But that didn't stop the intrepid Lord Brabazon when he visited the area in April to attend the opening of Hanson Transport's new depot. He looks rather frail and weary in this picture, and who can blame him, for the tiny flying machine, resembling a large insect, would have been cold, noisy (and probably terrifying!) as it made its way to the grounds of Norwood Grange, the home of Robert Hanson.

Above: April 1953, and the annual staff party for the staff at John Taylor's Mill is about to get under way. There *are* smiling faces among the tables - but you have to look really hard to find them! It's interesting to notice that the 'top table' with the management and directors seated upon it, is on the right of the picture. Of course, in 1953 it was usual to find that all the bosses were men, and the young men seen on the right of this picture were office boys and junior clerks who would one day train to be managers. Perhaps the ladies with the sombre expressions were impatient to get to grips with their boiled ham, or annoyed that only the top tables had flowers upon them? We may never know the reason for their sober appearance!

The room looks very well decorated and laid out for the staff, someone had obviously put a lot of thought into the arrangement of the tables and the food on the day. Let's hope everyone appreciated the effort and had an enjoyable party.

ROAD
ROLLERS
Limited
2021

Left: Chapel Hill was (and still is) a steep hill approaching a major road junction, so the local authority decided to install under-road heating to make the climb easier and safer during adverse weather conditions. The picture shows workmen resurfacing the road after laying the steel heating elements. The clock tower of the Co-op can be seen in the background, as can one of Huddersfield's trolley buses.

Below: The actual cables for the Chapel Hill under-road heating system are seen here, like the wires contained inside a giant electric blanket. Before the installation of the heating elements this slope, when covered with the lightest blanket of snow, was capable of preventing buses and lorries climbing the hill into the town centre. The delays and congestion that followed is easy to imagine.
Huddersfield followed the path taken by most other developing towns as the volume of road traffic increased in the 1950s. The pattern was similar virtually everywhere, the pressing task being to take the traffic out of the town centre, hence the creation of ring roads, and the building of multi-storey car parking facilities on the edge of the newly built shopping complexes. The aim of the planners was always to separate the shoppers from the motor vehicles in order to promote safety as well as a cleaner, more environmentally attractive, retail environment.

Above: This is how King Street looked in March 1966. The picture affords another reminder of how the Market Hall once stood proudly above the surrounding shops and streets, before the age of concrete and car parks began to change the townscape forever. By 1966 the new Boots store was already in place in King Street; of course, Wallaces Ltd., had traded from this spot for many years and their sign proclaiming 'quality' and 'service' had looked out on the street long before the concept was adopted by every other petrol station and burger bar in the country! The Kingsway cafe provided a calm oasis and popular meeting place above Wallaces long before anyone imagined that motor vehicles would eventually be barred from this street.
Before long the planners were to get the bright idea of creating hidden service-ways alongside, or, more often than not, below the modern shopping centres, so that deliveries could be made out of sight of the shoppers in the town. This would help keep disruption to a minimum and the cash ringing through the tills to a maximum.

"THE TOWER OF THE MARKET HALL ONCE STOOD PROUDLY OVER THE SURROUNDING SHOPS AND STREETS, BEFORE THE AGE OF CONCRETE AND CAR PARKS...."

F Beardsell & Son - building for success

This company was traditionally a joinery manufacturer but has now developed into a main contractor providing a wide range of construction services. The firm has been an active member of the Federation of Master Builders since 1967, became an NICEIC registered electrical contractor in 1991 and CORGI registered in 1995. In addition the firm is a member of three other trade associations and can therefore deal with most trades in-house and provide an excellent all-round service for its customers. The company was also a funeral director until Lawrence Beardsell retired in 1976. Four generations of the Beardsell family have now been involved in the business, all starting at the bottom and working their way up.

The company has a long history. It was in 1896-7 that two joiners, brothers Fred and William Beardsell, set up their own business. Ten years later, however, a split between them led to the birth of F. Beardsell & Son (Fred and his oldest son, Harold) based in a small workshop on Rashcliffe Hill in Huddersfield. A few years later, another son, Lawrence, became a partner, bringing the staff level up to five. The company remained for 41 years at these original premises in Rashcliffe Hill.

It has not been all plain sailing. Business was suspended during the Second World War. Later, just before Christmas in 1948, the workforce had finished logging but one of the saws had unbeknown become clogged with wet sawdust. The fire resulting from the spontaneous combustion from this residue

destroyed the whole premises. The death of Fred was a further tragedy at this time. The company pulled itself together and bought, refurbished and moved to its current premises, Spring Gardens, Lockwood.

Harold, who had hand made most of the company's original machinery, retired in 1965 and Lawrence bought him out, bringing in his own two sons, Ronnie and Raymond. During this partnership, F. Beardsell & Son bought one of their subcontractors, H. Pearson & Sons (Builders) Ltd.

In 1991 Nigel and Martin Beardsell were promoted to partners and in the same year Northern Electrical Contractors was purchased.

All company staff are trained to a high standard and there is a history of long and loyal service. One workshop foreman has been with F. Beardsell & Son longer than the current partners. The company has a wide range of clients- Century Inns, Burtonwood Brewery, Vaux, Bass Taverns, Mercedes Benz, Cowie Ford, grant maintained schools, medical practices and project designers as well as private individuals. Recent projects include the renovation of a large town centre building in Huddersfield for City Centre Restaurants Ltd.

Above: *Rashcliffe Hill in Huddersfield at the turn of the century. Fred Beardsell is in the centre of the photograph.* ***Top left:*** *Harold Beardsell, son of Fred and co-founder of the company.* ***Right:*** *Lawrence Beardsell.* ***Left:*** *The premises in Spring Gardens, Lockwood.*

Holset - an engineering heritage

The company was formed in 1952 as a member of the BHD group of companies in Turnbridge, Huddersfield. The company's title comes from the name of W.C.HOLmes company and the founding designer and first Managing Director, Louis CroSET.

Louis Croset was a Swiss engineer who designed the world's first ever flexible coupling in 1936 and joined the W.C. Holmes company to manufacture them. Flexible couplings for connecting rotating shafts and viscous dampers for reducing torsional vibration in engine crankshafts were the company's original product range.

Paul Croset, the son of Louis Croset, joined his father in 1952 and the business began on its present site in the building alongside the Worldwide technical Centre currently under construction. The turnover that year was £45,000 and the staff numbered 25. Rubber components were manufactured on site but castings and raw materials were purchased. The company grew rapidly during that decade, supplying prestigious diesel engine manufacturers like Rolls Royce and Sulzer and all the major steel works throughout England. Turbochargers were added to the product range in 1954, at first under license from the Swiss firm Buchi, though later Holset switched to an American design and was rewarded by orders from prestigious companies such as Volvo

1967 brought a setback when the manufacturing and office area of Bay 6 was destroyed by fire but the Holset workforce rose to the challenge and lived up to Holset's reputation for not letting the customer down.

In 1973 the company was acquired by the American diesel engine manufacturer Cummins Engine Company and five years later the millionth turbocharger was produced.

The eighties brought the establishment of Holset Manufacturing and marketing in the USA. The company acquired its former licensee in France, Dampers SA. The Aftermarket Division was established with worldwide headquarters also based in Huddersfield on the St. John's Road site.

In 1995 Holset formed an alliance with MHI to collaborate on turbocharger development. Sales increased to the leading manufacturers of medium to heavy duty diesel engines such as Cummins, Iveco, Scania, MAN, and RVI.

Wall displays in the factory's heritage Room take the interested visitor through the three successful decades of the company's history. Holset's future plans are to develop the Asian and Chinese markets through joint venture companies in these regions.

Above: *The Holset factory in the 1950s.* ***Top:*** *The original factory in Turnbridge, Huddersfield.* ***Left:*** *The same building seen in the 1950s.* ***Below:*** *Holset are proud of their association with local people and hold annual open-days to show the public 'just what it is that they do'.*

John Quarmby & Son Ltd - Bags of success!

Picture a man in a cloth cap trundling a hand cart round the streets of the West Riding in the 1870s. That was the genesis of the company that today has blue-chip standing in a customer base spanning breweries and airlines, oil companies and multi-nationals.

The man? John Quarmby. The contents of the handcart? Paper bags. Joe set up in Slaithwaite in 1872. His assets were one room doubling as office and warehouse, the cart for deliveries and determination. The last-named quality still motivates Quarmby's today as it uses the latest digital techniques on its ever-widening spectrum of products. Joe's bags deserved to be successful. He tested heavy-duty ones by filling them with bricks. Soon he took on a boy to make deliveries, in 1889 his elder son became a partner and by 1896, Joe was set up in 'proper' premises in Huddersfield and had bought his first bag-making machines. In 1906 his business became a limited liability company and moved to bigger premises, but on April 15th 1912, the day of the Titanic disaster, the factory was destroyed by fire. Joe rebuilt it. As part of his new start he decided to concentrate on the making of cardboard boxes.

The business continued to diversify, installing in 1931, plant for the manufacture of printed absorbent drip mats, a side line at first but quickly becoming a success. Now, overall, with products that include promotional clocks, screenprinting and the re-introduction of carton printing and manufacture, Quarmby's has a huge and disparate market. Five years ago, Quarmby's became part of Jarvis Porter and is now a leading member of the seven companies in the Group's IDB division. Quarmby is a distributor of promotional playing cards for Carta Mundi of Belgium and also tissue coasters, the only products they sell that they don't manufacture.

Old Joe Quarmby wouldn't recognise today's business as the one he founded so modestly but one thing is sure. It would take one of his extra-large and double-stitched bags to carry all the honours the company has gained since then.

Above: *The female workforce from the 1960s. Beehive hairstyles were just beginning to make their appearance.* ***Top:*** *An inside view of the factory.* ***Top left:*** *This van dates from the 1960s.* ***Left:*** *A slightly elevated view of the works.*

A foothold in Huddersfield's history

Everyone in Huddersfield is familiar with the retail outlets of this private limited company that was founded in 1864. In that year two businesses were established by John Shaw and Elliott Hallas respectively whose original activity was the making of the shoes.

In those days the leather was worked with hand tools. Mr Shaw had previously lived in Holmfirth where he had earned his living at lace making. Since then five generations of the family have served the business.

There were several changes of premises in the early days but no details can be found earlier than the period immediately prior to the First World War when the shop was in Westgate. By this time the two families had intermarried and combined their two businesses, forming a limited company. In 1923 a move was made to John William Street where the shop remained until 1961.

Like many another company, Shaw & Hallas experienced difficulties during the Second World War when customers were restricted by their

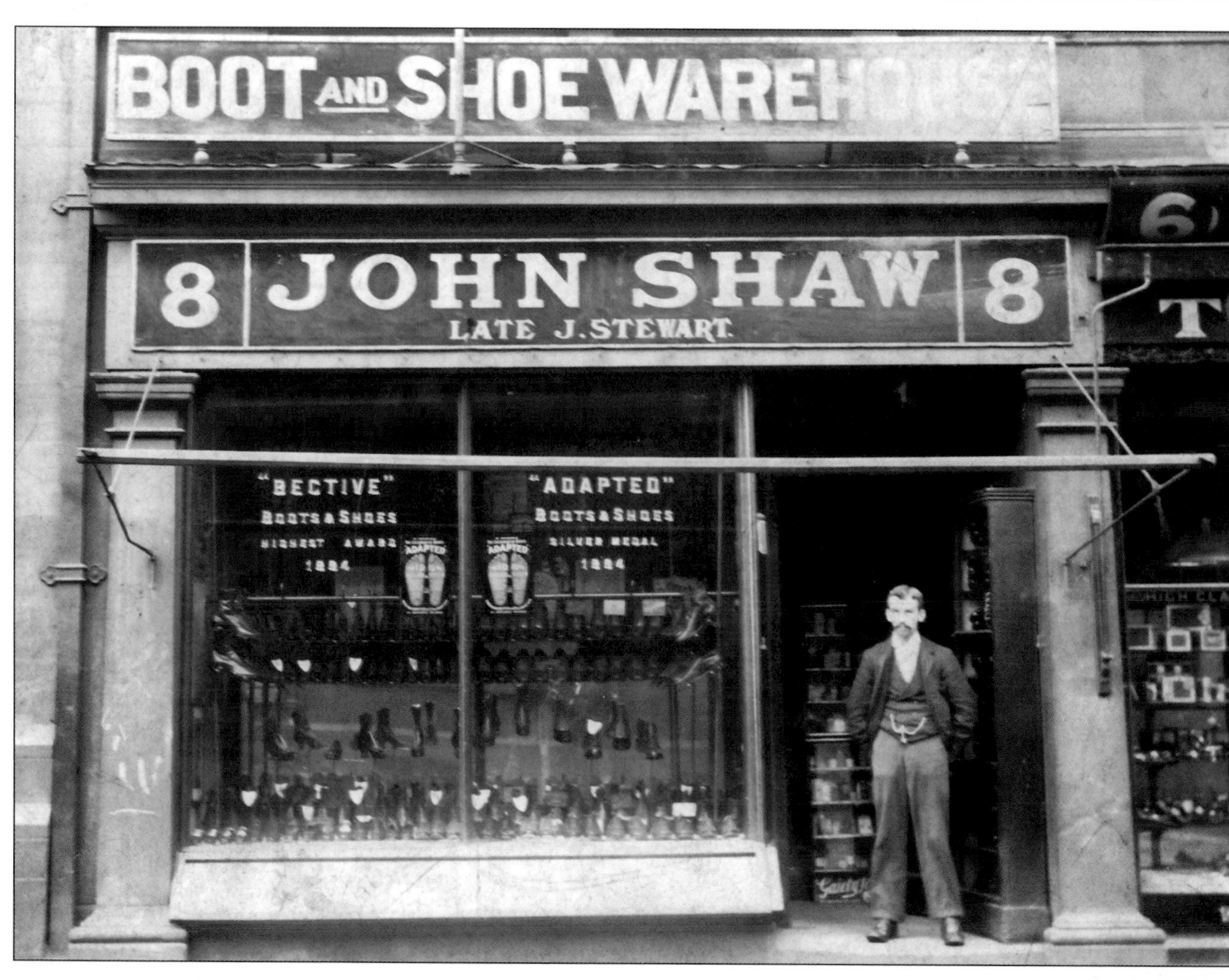

government coupons as to how many pairs of shoes they were allowed to buy. From time to time, 'Joyce' shoes would arrive from the USA on quota -when they were not lost at sea!- and these were snapped up with glee by the shoe starved ladies of Huddersfield.

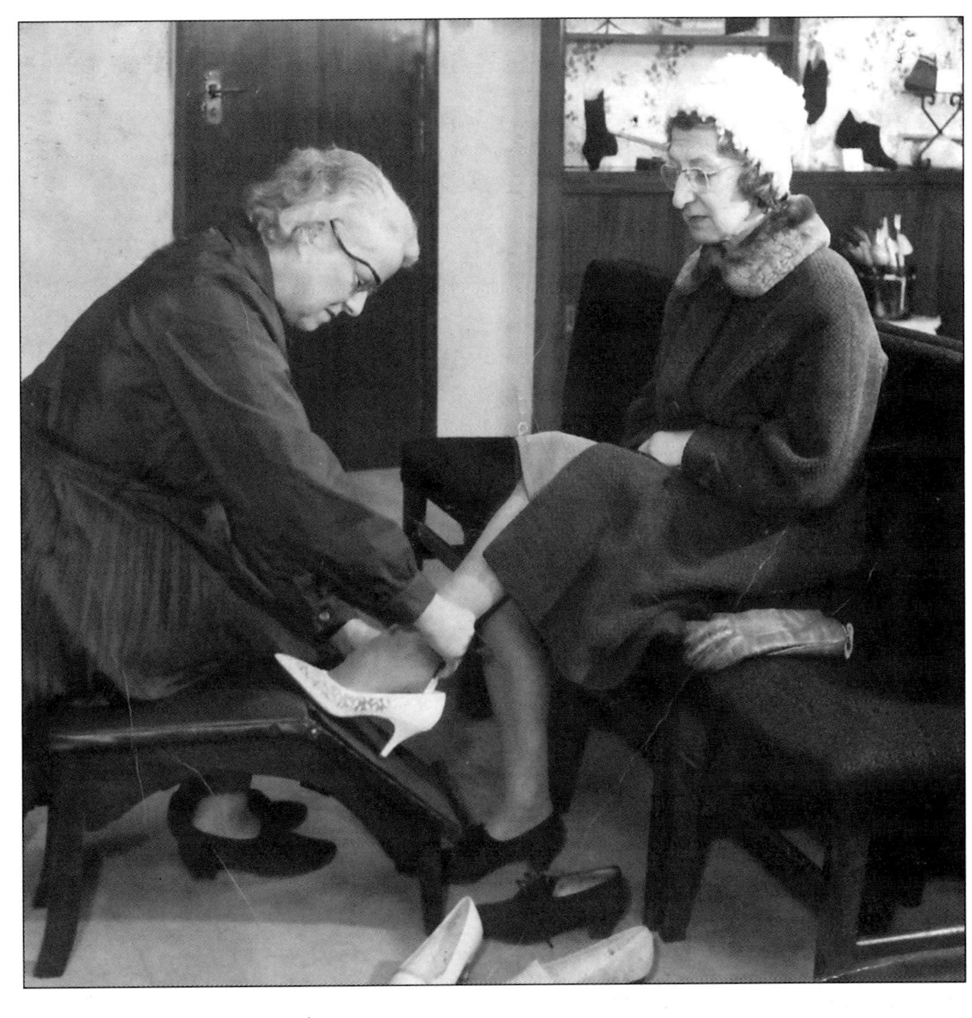

Shaw & Hallas modestly pride themselves on their 'fashion and fit' and their aim is 'to sell shoes that don't come back to customers who do'. They stock and sell only high quality footwear and carry a huge range of sizes and widths of shoes for men, women and children.

The staff have been trained to be knowledgeable about the merchandise and they use the latest technology to work out the correct fitting for each of their customers.

Still firmly based in Huddersfield, with the new premises on Market Walk, the company intends to maintain its unique quality and service whilst continually modernising their shop interior.

__Above:__ Pictured in the late 1960s, two members of staff, Sarah Barraclough (left) and Hilda Cox (right) posing as fitter and customer. __Facing page, bottom:__ Mr John Shaw taking the air outside the shop at number 8 Westgate. The year was 1889. The window signs are advertising 'Bective' boots and shoes which won an award in 1884 and 'Adapted' boots and shoes which were awarded a silver medal in the same year. Here the business calls itself a boot and shoe warehouse. The previous owner of the premises, one J Stewart, is acknowledged on the nameplate. __Facing page, top left:__ Mr John Shaw, lace maker of Holmfirth who switched to shoe making and was a co-founder of Shaw & Hallas (and inset) Mr. John Elliott Hallas who co-founded the company but about whom little else is known.

__Facing page, centre right:__ The premises at 12, Packhorse Walk where Shaw & Hallas had their premises from 1972-77

__Left:__ The premises at number 7, New North Road where Shaw & Hallas sold footwear from 1963-1966.

Wood Auto Supplies - A major force in the world of auto-electrics

A company that has been involved with auto-electrics for approximately 70 years, Wood Auto was founded in the 1920s by Reginald Wood who traded originally as 'Wood the Battery Man'. The first Certificate of Incorporation is dated 1929.

Reginald Wood was the youngest of a family of 14 children from Huntingdon. His earlier career as a munitions' inspector had brought him to Huddersfield.

Huntingdon was the home of Oliver Cromwell, and, although the company has moved its location over the years, it has always retained the address, "Cromwell Works". Reginald Wood was an influential force in the town and became Mayor of Huddersfield in the late fifties.

In the very early days, Reginald was assisted by his three daughters, Vera, Mollie and Peggy. The company began to specialise in rewinding automotive components and these skills were put to good use during the war years. After the war, Reginald's two sons, John and Walter, came back to Huddersfield, developing the merchandising side of the business.

The original firm had outgrown its premises and the winding operation was moved from Standard House to Portland Street, opposite the old Royal Infirmary. This business became Wood Auto Supplies Ltd. which concentrated on the manufacture of armatures, field coils, dynamos and starter motors. The company expanded under the direction of Douglas Heywood, who had been

one of Reginald's first apprentices when he left school in 1930, and John Wood. Meanwhile, John's younger brother, Walter, developed the Factoring division which today has branches in Leeds and Wakefield, as well as the main site on Colne Road, Huddersfield.

In a successful attempt to raise its profile, the company took a stand at the 1952 Motor Show. Export opportunities followed, the first orders coming from Australia and Turkey. The Wood Auto Supplies factory moved to Fitzwilliam Street in 1960, and again in 1980, to Colne Road, opposite the Wood Auto Factors branch. Today, Wood Auto Supplies exports to over 60 countries from Huddersfield.

Traditionally, the firm's products were aimed at British manufactured vehicles, but as the proportion of imported vehicles rose it diversified to meet the challenge. There are now over 7,000 parts in today's production range and since auto-electricians can no longer afford to keep large stocks, Woods does, offering both a van delivery and overnight courier service.

There are also depots in Glasgow, Belfast, Bristol and Bracknell and now subsidiary businesses in London and Italy. Wood Auto products are regularly fitted by such companies as Lucas, Valeo, Ford, Landrover, Case and Massey-Ferguson. Wood Auto is still a private independent company and the group today employs 150 people. Wood Auto believes that its knowledge of the trade is second to none. It has a proud history and a confident future.

Above: *A display at the 1952 Earl's Court Motor Show.* ***Facing page, top:*** *Reginald Wood, founder of the company.* ***Facing page, bottom:*** *The efficiency and skill of the workers is second to none and has always been an important factor in the success of the company.*

The self-made success story

In Huddersfield in 1903, two young men, without at the time realising it, were beginning to carve for themselves- and their successors- a niche in the history of the wool textile industry by forming a partnership to manufacture woollen and worsted cloth.

Frederick Louis Moorhouse and Charles William Brook commenced business as "Moorhouse & Brook". They had absolutely no equipment, so to begin with the cloth, from scribbling through to finishing, had to be made on commission.

Their first premises were at 8, Littlewoods Buildings. They rented one of the smallest and cleaned and decorated it themselves. Second hand furniture was bought and equipment rented from the National Telephone Company. A telegraphic address, Fibre Huddersfield, was registered and they were in business.

After four strenuous years working under pressure in cramped conditions, more commodious premises could be afforded in St. George's Square where the business remained for over 45 years. The town-centre location was a 'shop window' and the railway station was conveniently near.

To combat a rumour that M&B were merchants not manufacturers, the firm decided to commence their own manufacturing in nearby New Mill. They appointed a manager, Alfred Sykes, who soon had the new building operable. He was a stern disciplinarian and a great 'character'. Automatic looms were purchased which had previously been used only for cotton.

Meanwhile business at the warehouse in Huddersfield was expanding, where Mr Moorhouse was training boys to be salesmen. By 1913 the firm was becoming more widely known. Overseas markets were being served after visits made by Mr Brook who appointed foreign agents. Makers overseas were supplied in increasing quantities and, over the years export business has become a major part of the company's manufactures.

Above and top left: *Charles W. Brook and Fredrick L. Moorhouse, founders of the company.* ***Left:*** *St. George's Square.* ***Below:*** *A night time picture from the days before environmental control limited the amount of smoke pollution which was emitted into the air.*

This was the year in which Moorbrook Mills began to operate. The engine was named Marjorie after Mr Moorhouse's daughter. To celebrate the opening a gathering, with a meal and speeches was held in Lydgate School. Soon the business was in a position to employ its own representative in London. It opened its own office and showroom in Regency House, Golden Square, run by Harry Ewart Moorhouse, Mr Frederick's younger brother.

At this time, the total remuneration of the 17 employees was less than £20 a week. Most of the clerical work was hand-written but the requirements of foreign markets made it imperative to bring more typewriters into use. Even so, the handpress was used for copying documents like shipping advice notes. All mail for town addresses was delivered by hand.

All members of staff were encouraged to attend either the Technical College or evening classes to improve their knowledge of the wool textile trade, foreign languages and commercial subjects. Several members were awarded travelling scholarships under the auspices of the Huddersfield Chamber of Commerce. An innovation at Moorbrook Mills was the granting to operatives of quarter-hour breaks each morning and afternoon.

With the war, the making of civilian cloth stopped. At first the staff and work people were on a standing wage, half pay for half time work. When M&B eventually received their contract for 'Service Cloths' the workforce was recompensed generously.

Miles of service cloth, khaki and blue-grey, came from the looms, the 'making' side of the business following a routine whilst the selling side virtually ground to a halt.

Above: *A slightly elevated view of the mill in its surrounding moors taken in 1951.*
Below: *A gathering of the workers on May 1st 1918. This was six months before the end of the First World War and many of the women pictured here would hopefully soon be welcoming home husbands and sons.*

Harry Moorhouse was recalled to Huddersfield to help in St George's Square. Thomas Brook, Mr CW Brook's brother, was released from government work to help with M&B's production line. The main difficulty at the mill was labour. Replacements for the men who joined up were difficult to obtain.

In 1927 the firm purchased further factory premises in Huddersfield, and from this date was able to quote a vertical production system, carrying out all the processes of manufacture under its own control.

In the early 1930s the company started to expand into the men's overcoating market, which necessitated the installation of further production machinery at New Mill.

During the Second War the firm made uniform cloths. After the Armistice the company began an extensive building programme at New Mill which provided purpose-built accommodation for the manufacturing processes. It also allowed for the the company's offices and factory premises to be brought to New Mill from central Huddersfield, providing better control over the whole manufacturing operation.

At this time, the business began to produce coatings using speciality hairs, -cashmere, camel and alpaca- which increased the company's revenue. Serges and baratheas having become less popular, their manufacture was gradually discontinued.

1953 marked not only the Golden Jubilee of the firm but also the removal to Moorbrook Mills of the registered office and the warehouse. Some of the longest-serving employees were sceptical concerning the removal, considering that to have the warehouse in the town centre was an arrangement not to be improved upon.

However, all proved to be for the best. New conditions in the general office were admirable. Staff who had worked on high desks on tall stools now each had a desk of his own with a modern chair. Their chief discomfort was noise. After a while, electric typewriters arrived but a noiseless loom was too much to ask for.

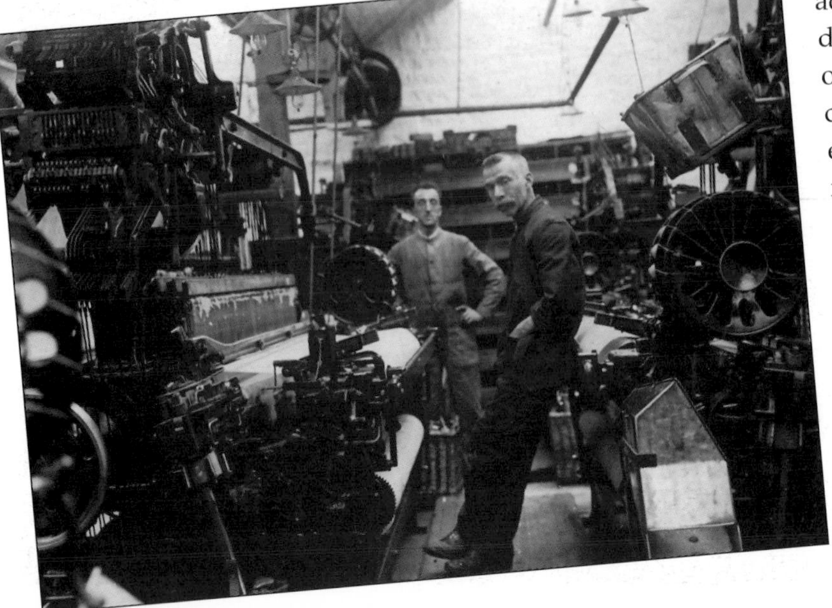

Above and top left: *Two works 'occasions', both dating from the 1940s.*
Left: *Joe Marshall, the head tuner talking to Norman Bray (at the end of the loom). Mr Marshall began work for M&B in 1913 for 15s a week. Mr Bray began service in September 1917.*

On October 26th 1955 M&B was incorporated as a private company under the name B&M (Textiles) Ltd. and in this year the night shift was discontinued. April 1956 brought another change of name, this time to Moorhouse & Brook Ltd..

In 1960 the decision was taken to move the finishing plant to Moorbrook Mills. This involved an alteration to the 'Old' Mill to accommodate the 'Wet' finishing and the erection of a new building for the 'dry' processes. This new plant commenced operations in 1962 and the very last one-shuttle loom was scrapped. At about the same time Moorhouse & Brook went public.

In July 1966, M&B made tentative enquiries about Alex Begg (Woollen Manufacturers) Ltd. of Ayr which they acquired two years later. The seventies saw the replacement of much equipment, together with innovations such as the vending machine for the convenience of the staff. In January 1979 came the announcement of the Scheme of Arrangement for the formation of a new company, Yorklyde Ltd.

It came into being in July as the ultimate holding company for Moorhouse & Brook Ltd., Alex Begg & Company Ltd. and Lockwood & Keighley Ltd. Currently, Arthur Bell (Scotch Tweeds), William Edleston, Robert Noble, Replin Fabrics and Westcountry Clothing are also part of the concern.

Under the Yorklyde umbrella all the companies are independently managed as they have been since being founded as family firms.

Moorhouse & Brook is still in the control of the members of the two families who founded it over 90 years ago. While the firm has kept abreast of modern methods of manufacture and marketing, and in communications, one thing has remained constant, their policy of perfection. It is what the company has always aimed at and what it has achieved.

Above: *A 1950s office scene.*
Below: *New Mill surrounded by the beautiful rolling hills around Huddersfield.*

Quarmby & Sykes - waste not, want not!

James Quarmby and James Sykes established their business in 1868. Five years later, on 1st September 1873, they leased the Dyehouse Reservoir and Cottages at Cowlersley in Linthwaite where they dealt in flock and waste and extracting oil from textile waste which was collected by workers on foot.

There was a continuation of the lease at Linthwaite in 1887 where the company remained until 1895. During that year there was an official partnership agreed between John Quarmby and Freddie Sykes, sons of the founders, and a further move was made to Spinksmire Mill at Meltham where woollen manufacturing wastes were processed by garnets and rag grinding machines. Here the grandparents of Peter Sykes and John Quarmby, the present joint managing directors, installed the first electric lights in Meltham.

Under the direction of John Quarmby and Freddie Sykes a new steam engine was bought in 1896 to drive the machines in this new factory. It was christened 'Her Majesty' and caused great excitement because its capabilities included the new one of driving a dynamo to generate sufficient electricity to light up 50 electric bulbs in the factory and its office.

Mr Peter Sykes still has the brass plate from this steam engine. The engine itself has been donated to the museum of the Northern Mill Engine Society in exchange for a promise to re-erect it.

On 19th February 1902, Quarmby & Sykes became a limited company. There was increased activity during the war to supply uniform cloths. The government must have been pleased to have cloth which through this early form of recycling could be produced so cheaply.

Above: *The management in 1936: from left to right, Mr Edward Sykes, Mr Alec Quarmby and Mr P Matthews.*
Below: *Wool and cotton fibres are sorted for recycling.*

In a catalogue from 1936 the company describe themselves as 'Manufacturers of Wool Wastes, Extracts, Mungoes, Merinoes, Stockings, etc. Carbonizers and Dyers.' Mungoes were low grade waste fibres recovered by pulling down old hard-woven woollen rags such as felt.

Merinoes were wool fibres recovered from fine woollen and worsted clothing rags. The carbonizing process meant steeping wool in a dilute solution of sulphuric acid or hydrochloric acid gas (the dry process). This converted the cellulosic impurities to carbon dust which was easy to dispose of. The company did not and still does not supply a finished product but currently supply dyed yarns to apparel and upholstery weavers.

In November 1971 the company bought package yarn dyers Edwin Brook & Company Ltd. of Honley. By 1980 the decision was taken to move most of the machinery to Spinksmire Mill in Meltham, and ten years later Quarmby and Sykes Ltd. ceased fibre reclamation and specialised solely in the field of yarn merchanting and package yarn dyeing. There is further modernisation in progress. Part of the old site has been leased to another business as new technology means that the work can be done in less space. After almost 130 years of success Quarmby & Sykes can look forward to a future equally as bright.

Above: *The original dyehouse pictured here being used in 1936 is still going strong, although the premises have been completely modernised to incorporate new machinery.*
Left: *The warehouse at Spinksmire Mill in 1936.*
Top: *The pulling department 1936.*

From a class of five to a national centre for learning

In May 1841, five young men, employed and encouraged by Frederic Schwann, a German merchant who ran an export business in Huddersfield, met in a temperance hotel in Cross Church Street and set up a Young Men's Mental Improvement Society. Joined by about thirty others, they began night classes in the British and Foreign Society's school in Outcote Bank, taught by a mixture of paid and voluntary teachers.

It was renamed the Mechanics' Institution, financed by subscriptions and fees and, from 1844, organised by a paid secretary and guided by an elected committee. By 1850 its reputation was high because it taught not 'science' to 'mechanics' but the three Rs to illiterate young men and boys.

The character of the Institution was moulded by a few able men devoted to the ideal of service to others. Among them were Frederic Schwann himself, George Phillips, Frank Curzon and George Jarmain.

Jarmain taught Chemistry for 30 years from 1864 and established the link which tied the college to the town's chemical and dyeing industries. Pressures had converged to shift the emphasis of teaching from elementary education to scientific and technical subjects. The 1870 Education Act meant schools had to take over the three Rs.

In 1884 the Technical School and Mechanics' Institution moved into a new building in Queen Street South. It had flourished through the generous support of the Ramsden family whose coat of arms was on the facade of the building.

During the 1890s the Technical College - so renamed in 1896 - was chronically short of money, so that in 1903 control passed to Huddersfield County Borough Council.

By 1914 the College had an annual income of nearly £13,000 and was teaching about 1,800 students, ranging in level from final honours of London University to day release classes for apprentices. It had a well-patronised public reading room, a library of 9,000 volumes and a museum that provided a service to schools whose teachers it helped to train.

Above: *The Mechanics Institute from the turn of the century.*
Left: *During the Second World War the University housed many female student teachers. This chemistry class from that period shows a lone woman amongst many young men.*

The 1914-18 war stimulated growth in the college as a direct result of the government's formation of British Dyes Ltd. Local donations funded research scholarships, the basis of the college's reputation for chemical research. The generosity of Huddersfield textile employers largely funded the new buildings for the Textile and Dyeing Departments.

Student numbers rose during the inter-war years. Then, during the second world war the college housed women student teachers evacuated from London, members of the armed services and civilians on crash courses in basic workshop skills.

In the fifties and sixties the mood swung between elation and despair. In 1953 Huddersfield Council resolved to clear the site for extensive new building, hoping the college would become a College of Advanced Technology but Bradford was chosen in 1957.

By 1966, however, a White Paper announced the names of proposed polytechnics, Huddersfield amongst them. The proposal was confirmed in 1967. Huddersfield Polytechnic was inaugurated in June 1970. It merged Huddersfield College of Technology with Oastler College of Education. It was enlarged in 1974 by the absorption of Huddersfield College of Education which had moved to its own premises in the Edgerton district in 1958 and in 1974 occupied an extensive campus at Holly Bank.

***Above:** A class from the 1950s.* ***Right:** The former Technical School and Mechanics' Institution Building, Queen Street South, opened in 1883.*

Much physical expansion has been in response to increasing student numbers which doubled between 1970 and 1990. In 1989 the Polytechnic became a self-governing body, independent of the Local Education Authority. In the summer of 1992, along with all the former polytechnics, it was granted university status.

What started as a philanthropic 'self-help' group in Victorian times is now a thriving university with eight Schools and some 15,000 full-time and part-time students. The University remains committed to Pennine West Yorkshire but has strong national and international links. It prides itself on its enviable record for graduate employment and is well known for hosting the annual Contemporary Music Festival. The Music Department is one of the biggest in the country - appropriate for a university in a town with such a strong musical tradition.

A remarkable story of achievement in Huddersfield

In 1817, Benjamin Crook established a small leather tannery. Nearly 200 years later, as Mitre Sports International Ltd., the same company is known the world over for its sporting goods and footwear and its footballs are used wherever the game is played. The casual buyer has little understanding of the exacting standards to which the manufacture of sports equipment is working. The strictest attention is paid to the official weights and measurements specified by each sports' governing body.

Mitre, originally known as Benjamin Crook & Sons, began using its expertise in leather for soccer and rugby in the 1880s when the games were becoming established. The exact location of the premises is not known but it is certain that the company tanned on site. All balls were made from leather. Nowadays leather is only used in the manufacture of football and rugby boots and trainers. Balls are made

Above: *This picture dating from the 1930s, shows the procedure of hand-stitching balls. This method has been tried and tested over the years and today, is still the most effective and popular.*
Left: *A stall in Huddersfield Market.*
Below: *Raw hides which were received in the cellar. The picture dates from the early 1930s.*

from a variety of man-made materials including PU and PVC.

Over the years, through acquisitions and expansions, Mitre widened its activities to include the manufacture at various times of squash, badminton and tennis racquets, Billiard tables, golf clubs and fitness equipment, besides balls, bags and cricket gear.

In the 1960s, Grampian Holdings, a Scottish group with a portfolio of sports companies, acquired Mitre and the subsequent expansion saw the company add sports footwear manufacturing to its other activities and plunged Mitre into exporting.

In 1978 Mitre overflowed the premises it had occupied for more than a hundred years and moved to larger ones, nearby and still in Birkby. The company completely reorganised its manufacturing operations, transferring to one location all the footwear, accessories, cricket, soft leather bags, ball preparation and stitching operations. The reorganisation was completed without losing the unique core of expert craftsmen which assured Mitre's quality

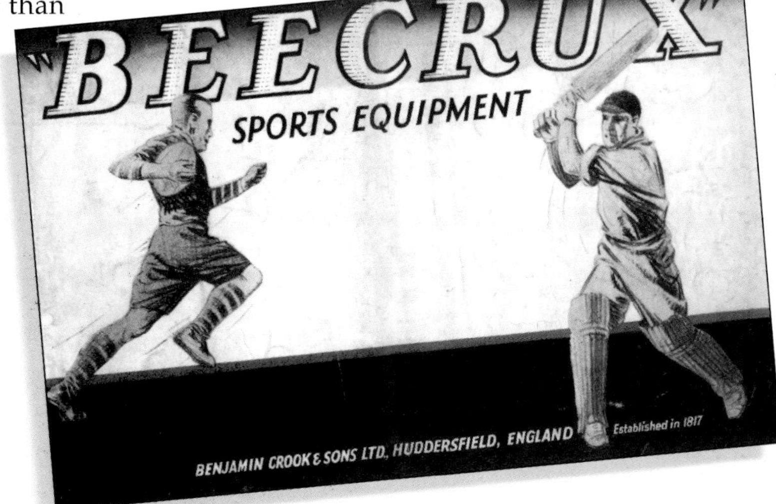

1981-82 saw Mitre in an unprecedented position in its home market. Ninety per cent of English and one hundred per cent of Scottish Professional League Clubs played Mitre exclusively during that season and all four British Cup Finals as well as all English, Scottish and Irish internationals were played with Mitre balls. Their domination of the UK soccer scene continues to this day.

The company has a full time development team on balls, constantly investigating materials, construction, bounce, durability and flight characteristics. The launch of Mitre's distinctive Delta-designed ball in 1984 has resulted in ever-increasing sales. With this history and its current resources and expertise, Mitre looks forward to the future.

Top: *Men softening the hides with fat liquor and sperm whale oil in the 1930s.*
Above centre: *A brochure dating from the same period with a staggering array of footballs on display within its pages.*
Left: *The premises in Birkby as seen in the 1960s.*

Garrards - the oldest timber company in Huddersfield

This business was set up in 1917 by Mr Stanley Garrard and a Mr Eastwood whose forename is not known. At their premises in Great Northern Street, where the company still flourishes today, their original activity was the construction of ammunition boxes for the war. Mr Eastwood's connection with the firm lasted only 2-3 years and there is no record of his subsequent activities.

Mr Stanley Garrard, on the other hand, stayed with his company until his well-earned retirement, which he spent on the Isle of Man. The business, which was housed in Great Northern Street, was taken over by his son Geoffrey. Under his chairmanship it continued to flourish.

With the advent of the Second World War, the company returned to its original purpose and function, making packing cases for ammunition. Like all firms, they lost some of their men to the armed services and their work force in the office began to contain more women.

Mr Derek Stott was his managing director and it was Mr Stott who held the fort when Geoffrey Garrard died in a tragic drowning accident. Mr Garrard's favourite relaxation had been sailing his boat which was kept on Windermere and he and his family had been on holiday there when the tragedy occurred.

The Garrards had four children, but the eldest was only 15. In the absence of a suitable family

member to take immediate control Mr Stott held the business in trust.

Soon it was discovered that death duties were going to make for difficult times. Mr Stott therefore bought the Garrards out and went on running Garrards as its owner.

At this time Garrards suffered a setback in the form of a serious fire. It occurred during a night when the Huddersfield brigade had to deal with four fires in two hours. An estimated £3,000 worth of damage was caused to the hardwood store and its contents. Delayed by a small fire at Scarbottom Mills in Milnsbridge, the firemen arrived to find flames leaping through the roof. Despite the severe damage, the fire was prevented from spreading to other timber stores.

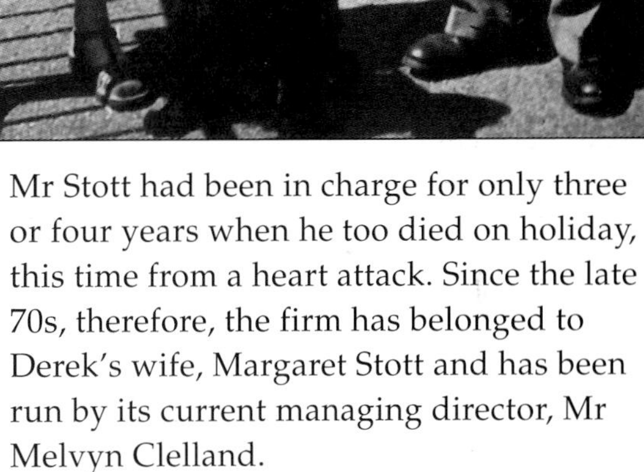

Mr Stott had been in charge for only three or four years when he too died on holiday, this time from a heart attack. Since the late 70s, therefore, the firm has belonged to Derek's wife, Margaret Stott and has been run by its current managing director, Mr Melvyn Clelland.

Garrards seldom sees the goods that its containers are to be used for. Its customers specify the dimensions and materials required and the company delivers the finished containers.

Above: *Geoffrey Garrard with his wife pictured here in the early 1960s.*
Left: *Garrards took part in this parade during the 1950s, honouring the efforts of the soldiers in the First World War. Pictured over the cab is a painting of the men 'going over the top'. The event as well supported, the crowds lined the route seven deep and cheered as the vans and floats went by.*
Far left: *A page from the company's DIY catalogue dating from 1969. At the time their most expensive ladder cost nearly £11.*

Sometimes they go the second mile. For example, when the United States were taking military action against Libya in the early 70s and there was an embargo on exports there from the UK, Garrards offered storage facilities to one of their customers. The customers' business was the production of desalination plants to the Middle East and their equipment had overflowed their own storage space as they waited for the government embargo to be lifted.

Garrards have remained in their premises on Great Northern Street for all their 80 years. However, as the company's business has grown they have acquired and moved into neighbouring buildings.

When they took over the boiler company, Alan Knight, the building had to be cleared of huge pieces of equipment including whole boilers and steam rollers, before the place could be demolished and completely rebuilt. A further plot of land, which had contained 50 houses was cleared by the council before the company acquired it.

One of the present managing director's least pleasant experiences was, accompanied by a policeman and his tracker dog, finding the body of the Yorkshire Ripper's 13th victim.

Garrards work chiefly with timber and plywood to make cases, crates and pallets of any size the customer requires. However, an important aspect of their business is selling DIY equipment to Huddersfield householders. As is fitting for the oldest timber company in Huddersfield, Garrards has earned customer satisfaction through applying skilled craftsmanship to good quality materials according to its individual customers' requirements.

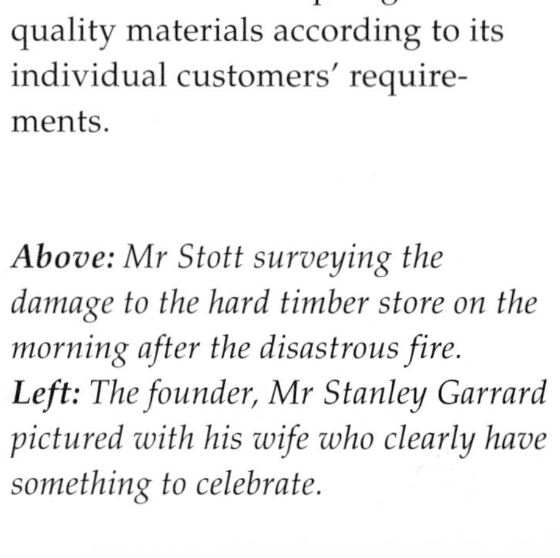

***Above:** Mr Stott surveying the damage to the hard timber store on the morning after the disastrous fire.*
***Left:** The founder, Mr Stanley Garrard pictured with his wife who clearly have something to celebrate.*

A 'simple action' that changed the world

Cliffe & Co, manufacturers of textile and loose fibre handling machinery, was established in 1900 and is now a private Limited Company. The management describe themselves as 'Masters in the Art of Moving and Handling Loose Fibre'.

Their first claim to fame was on February 15th 1887, when the venerable 'Textile Recorder' featured an Automatic Feed Apparatus for Scribblers made by Cliffe and Co., Longwood, Huddersfield. The publication described the problem it solved. "....it is so difficult to get a human feeder who is always reliable that the use of some sort of mechanism for the purpose is imperative."

The apparatus was designed to feed the wool or worsted without the necessity for careful placing of the wool in the feed box. It consisted of a box placed on a bracket at the back of the scribbler. The box was triangular in section. Along the sloping side was an endless feed sheet with teeth, that passed over two pulleys.

Stock was placed in the box and the motion of the sheet caused the teeth to pull out portions of fibre. A comb regulated the quantity of wool and a vibrating brush removed it after the sheet had passed round the upper roller.

The Textile Recorder was approving. "The whole action is simple- no parts are liable to get out of order."

All this is a far cry from the company's activities today, producing spiked and lattice sheets and machinery, designing and building it and then repairing, maintaining and modifying it as required by their modern customers.

The machines are used worldwide, being exported to Europe, North America, Australasia and the Middle and Far East. Nevertheless, modern promotional material remind all customers that 'Old Cliffe' had the knowledge.

Above: *An atmospheric picture dating from the 1960s with a lone man just visible in the doorway of Cliffe's premises. Beside him is a bike, obviously his transport to and from work!* ***Top:*** *The workforce from the 1940s.* ***Above left:*** *An automatic feed apparatus dating from the 1880s. It was advertised in a textile journal.* ***Left:*** *The deserted yard and long shadows indicates that it was evening sometime in the early 1950s. One could date the picture earlier but for the top of a Morris Minor van in the background.*

Shaw Son & Greenhalgh - the local company with worldwide connections

Joseph Shaw & Company was originally founded in 1876, operating as a brass foundry and general engineers from premises at Alma Works. The company's registered offices were at Springfield Mills (now Albert Works) which it acquired at auction in 1893 from a Mr. E.S. Hilton, Scribbler & Waste Operator. Since 1893 land and buildings have gradually been acquired on the town side of Springfield Mills.

In May 1912 the company acquired the Economic Gas Company Ltd. During both world wars a large part of the company's production was turned over to munitions.

Immediately after the First World War the company was manufacturing the 'Universal Gas Wash Boiler' under the name of the Torpedo Washer Company. The price of a number 1 with extra powerful burner and 12 gallon capacity was 40 shillings in 1923.

In 1926 William Calvert Shaw and James Greenhalgh succeeded Joseph Shaw on his death as joint managing directors.

In 1936, the Bay Horse Hotel was bought from Wilson's Brewery (formerly Seth Senior & Sons of Shepley) and converted into

The Greenhalgh family interest in the business was strengthened in 1909. James Greenhalgh became a director on an annual salary of £156 per annum! He had joined J. Shaw & Company in 1893 at the age of 15 and served for a total of 70 years.

Above: *The workforce from the turn of the century.* ***Top:*** *A letterhead dating from around the same time.* ***Right:*** *An early method of transportation, one of the first motorised vehicles to supersede the horse.*

were converted to house the company's non-ferrous foundry and, during that work a deep well was discovered. It is believed to have been a sulphur well that was connected with the Old Lockwood Spa.

The company continued to expand and between 1951 and 1958 new buildings were erected to house the machine shops which are still in use today. The name officially changed to Shaw Son & Greenhalgh on 18th February 1964.

Originally the company manufactured governors for the gas industry but gradually it began to make valves and, since 1919 it has specialised entirely in this field. The company's range of valves and

offices and is still used as the company's main offices today.

It was not until 1942 that the company was finally able to acquire Bintley & Tate's premises including the section of land down to the river, to increase the area of the site to its present size.

In 1941, W.C. Shaw died and the company became wholly owned by the Greenhalgh family. Then, Donald Ramsden Greenhalgh and James Kenneth Greenhalgh (sons of James) were appointed directors. The present joint managing directors, Malcolm James Greenhalgh and Martin Greenhalgh are the grandsons of James. In 1947 Lockwood Baths were purchased from Huddersfield Borough Council for £5,100. They

fittings for all types of steam boilers were specifically tailored to the requirements of the textile industry and has developed further from there. Whilst the company still manufactures this type of equipment it is moving into the more sophisticated area of controlling hazardous chemicals and has recently received the Queen's Award for the Environment for working in this field. It is a product that is relevant to all countries in the world as a consequence of which, exports have risen sharply.

It is interesting to note that the only connection the company has with its original product is their telegraphic address - 'Governor - Huddersfield.'

Above: *The machine room from the 1920s.*
Top: *The office from the Second World War.*
Left: *Another view of the workshop from the turn of the century.*

The English Card Clothing Company
July 1897 - July 1997

The first thing Chairman Nicholas Joseph Sykes Walker points out to uninitiated visitors to the Company is that it does not either make or sell garments. The clothing in the title refers to the clothing of the carding machine which is used to process fibres. 'Carduus' is Latin for thistle or teazle. The prickly heads of the teazle were once used to tease the wool or cotton until it formed silk-like slivers that could be spun. Raw cotton or wool straight from the sheep comes in bales of tangled fibres. It cannot be spun until the fibres have been straightened or 'carded' and Joseph Sykes Bros, a founder company of ECC, was originally set up to produce machinery to perform this process.

John Sykes of Lindley was the founder of the firm which became known as Joseph Sykes Brothers. When he died his three elder children, Joseph (20), John(18) and William (15) were rather young to take the business over. His widow Charlotte however was an astute businesswoman, more than capable of rearing her large family at the same time as running her husband's firm. Renaming it Charlotte Sykes and Sons, in 1833 she had Acre Mills built on her husband's land at a cost of £6,500. Correspondence from that time shows that pricking and card making were still separate operations and the complete card setting machine had not yet been adopted.

In 1845 the partnership of Charlotte Sykes and Sons was dissolved and Charlotte handed over the whole stock in trade, valued at £4,539, to her three elder sons. Trading as Joseph Sykes Brothers the business continued to prosper and they were soon able to repay her from their profits. Later the youngest son, James Nield Sykes was taken into the firm.

Up to this time the business had had its own tannery because leather was the base for the steel teeth which combed the wool and cotton as it passed over the steel cylinders of the machines. From 1855, Joseph Sykes Brothers began making up foundations for the cards using rubber cement instead but the tannery continued until the late fifties.

In 1865, Joseph died, leaving no children to inherit his estate. Some nine years later, therefore, William Sykes was able to bring in his only son, Frederick William who

responsibility, introducing improvements and innovations and becoming first chairman of the English Card Clothing Company from its formation in 1897 until he died in 1914

Meanwhile, in 1870, brothers George and Elijah Ashworth had patented a process of flattening wire by passing it through hardened steel rollers. The card clothing company used it for a short time.

In 1878 Ashworths patented a process for hardening steel wire in a continuous length. Two years later Sykes Brothers patented the same process by a different method. Ashworths sued Sykes for infringement and litigation continued for four and a half years. In 1903, eventually became the second chairman of ECC. Frederick William married in 1891. His wife, the former Catherine Whiteley, was the great granddaughter of John Whiteley, founder of Messrs John Whiteley and Sons, another major card clothing business, so two very old card making families were united. In 1843, the couple produced a grandson for Charlotte, another John. The boy was sent as apprentice to Platt Brothers of Oldham to learn about cotton textile machinery, then visited India before coming back to work for his uncles. He was paid £1 a week for managing the spinning business at Acre Mills.

When John had proved himself, he was given the card business to manage as well. He thrived on the

Above: *Flat grinding of cotton flats.* ***Top:*** *Wire testing in the laboratory at Lindley.* ***Left:*** *Fillet grinding at Cleckheaton using the same process as the above picture.* ***Facing page, top centre:*** *Acre Mills, Lindley as seen at the turn of the century.* ***Facing page, bottom left:*** *'Filling up and inspection'. Putting teeth in by hand after setting.*

when the House of Lords decided for Sykes there was a celebratory dinner for all their employees.

Big changes followed William's death in 1881. World trade increased enormously, with America, India and Japan, particularly in cotton. Electric light was introduced and Acre Mills was enlarged to become the largest cotton card manufacturing plant in the world. In 1892 the firm converted into a private limited company and soon afterwards the great grandson of the founder, Edward Sykes joined his firm.

In 1897 The English Card Clothing Company Ltd. was formed by Joseph Sykes Brothers, the owners of Whiteleys together with Samuel Law and Sons which had been established by the Law Family in 1816. Wilson and Ingham had been started by William Wilson who became a director of ECC from its inception. He had founded Wilson & Ingham at Hightown near Anderton's silk works on Pancake Tuesday 1881. John Sykes was chairman of the new company which traded with Russia, America, Canada, India and Japan. Over the next year or two, the company acquired Crosland & Whiteley Ltd. and James Walton & Son Ltd. In 1903 it was resolved to build a new grinding shed at Lindley which became J. W. & H. Platt's main metallic wire shed in 1972.

To mark John Sykes' ten years as chairman of ECC, the directors held a dinner after the 1907 AGM at which a large portrait of himself in oils was presented to him Also in that year, the company bought Edwin Stead & Sons of Cleckheaton, binding the services of Stead's two nephews to run it to make card setting machines for them. In 1911 ECC branched out into the manufacture of iron wire and became in time the third largest producer of it in the country. During the Great War, the government used it in planes and munitions.

1915 brought a strike, the first and last 100% one in the history of the industry in Yorkshire and Lancashire. The cost of living had increased by 35% between July 1914 and December 1915 and employers had refused to raise wages by 15%. It lasted until May 1916. Thereafter relations improved and ECC's board decided to give employees £50 for 50 years' continuous service. In 1938, holidays with pay were granted in principle, finally being implemented in July 1939. In the same year the company decided to make up the pay of their staff who had been drafted into the forces to what the company would have been paying them throughout the war with additions for rises. They were rewarded for this generous gesture when most of the work force returned to them after demobilisation.

After the war ECC shares were offered to the public and it was registered as a public limited company. Its range of business by now included the manufacture of all kinds of card clothing and its components, card foundations in cloth and leather, card wire, abrasive wheels and materials and iron and steel wire for its own use and for sale.

There was a worldwide and continuing demand for the company's products from every industry concerned with textiles and other products. In 1946 Acre House at Lindley became the centre for the administration of all operations. There was pressure on the order books as mills replaced worn out card clothing and the firm was glad of its returned workforce but still inconvenienced by fuel and power restrictions and the scarcity of raw materials, especially steel.

It was decided in 1967 to stop flexible card making at Lindley and to transfer it to Cleckheaton. As part of a programme of consolidation, new offices were constructed at Acre Mills and in 1971 the board decided that the growing activities of ECC's subordinate company, Platts in Harrow, should be transferred to Lindley. Adequate space was available and the workers there had experience of making metallic card clothing. An increase in production followed the move to Huddersfield and the business has continued to grow to meet world demand,to such an extent that ECC moved en bloc in September 1993 to the larger premises at Plover Mill next door.

Above: *The wire patenting line at Lindley.* ***Left:*** *Chairman, Nicholas Walker with one of the company's service vans in 1994.* ***Facing page, top:*** *Foundation manufacture on the Vulcanising press, dating from the 1960s.* ***Facing page, bottom:*** *Automatic card setting machinery from around the same period.*

The company with its eye on the 'Horizon'

Sellers & Company is a long-established, independent firm which is fully equipped to carry out a wide variety of light and medium engineering tasks. The company's core business lies in the design and manufacture of machinery for textile finishing processes. Current turnover approaches £10 million, of which 70% is in exports.

The company was founded by Mr. Arthur Edwin Sellers on December 15th 1912 in Huddersfield as Sellers & Co and the home town connection remains to the present day. It was registered in London in May 1925 when the name Sellers & Company (Huddersfield) Ltd. was adopted.

Mr. Arthur Edwin Sellers had been a partner in the textile machinery business of Thewlis, Sellers & Co, founded in 1909 which operated out of Phoenix Works, Folly Hall, Huddersfield, but the partnership was dissolved in December 1912.

Not a great deal is known of the early days of the firm, save that it specialised from the start in the design and manufacture of textile machinery for local cloth producers. According to an advertisement in the Yorkshire Textile Directory for 1913-14 its business was "Dyeing and Finishing Machinery for Woollen & Worsted Clothes, Plushes, Sealskins, Carpets etc."

The business began on the present site known as Engine Bridge Machine Works off Chapel Hill. The premises had earlier been a Woollen Dyehouse called Engine Bridge Dyehouse.

During the First World War, production was diverted to the manufacture of mines for the Admiralty.

By the 1930s, when Arthur Sellers' two sons Eric and Leo joined the business, the Sellers name was known nationally. Photographs and brochures from that period illustrate an extensive range of textile machinery in the manufacturing programme. Arthur was then managing director. Eric undertook

Above: *Making wheels for Lancaster and Halifax Bombers during the Second World War.*
Left: *Cement Hollow Block making c1950.*

sales whilst Leo was involved in the workshop and its management. They worked mainly with lathes, drills and a planer on cast iron, brass, steel and timber.

Whilst Mr. A.E. Sellers was building up his successful business, he was also actively involved in local civic life. A Justice of the Peace, he was elected Mayor of Huddersfield from 1940-41.

During the Second World War, production was again directed to the war effort, this time under the control of Dunlop Rim and Wheel. The work force, containing a high proportion of female operatives, made wheel assemblies for bomber aircraft such as the Lancaster and the Halifax.

At the end of the 1940s, Mr. R.F. (Eric) Sellers, the son of the founder, had taken over the position of managing director, and he was instrumental in putting the sales of Sellers' machinery on an international footing. He and his sales team travelled extensively to promote the company's products and now as we approach the end of the century Sellers & Company has machinery in over 60 countries world-wide.

Eric Sellers was, for example, one of the first British businessmen to visit Moscow after the Second World War in 1953, as part of an official delegation. His foresight was rewarded some three years later by receipt of orders totalling some £15 million -a huge undertaking at that time. Recent contacts with the former USSR confirm that the majority of this machinery is still operating efficiently 40 years later.

Mr Arthur Sellers died in January 1954 aged 73. Less than two years later the premature death of Leo left Eric with full control and responsibility.

Above: *(Left to right) Eric Sellers with his father, the founder, Arthur Sellers.*
Top: *An advert taken from the 'Cotton Yearbook' dating from 1920.*
Above left: *Metal pouring in the 1950s.*
Below: *The main assembly shop from around the same period.*

Aided Design system has been integrated into the Drawing Office. One of their latest ventures has been the introduction of machinery for processing carpet tiles - coating, cutting, trimming and shearing.

General Engineering is now playing a steadily increasing role in Sellers' activities. They supply 'special' machinery for a variety of jobs, for example Pea-Picking machines, Post Office Sorting Tables, Tennis Ball Coating Equipment, a Mesh Cutting and Baling machine and Packaging Machines for the Food and Beverage Industries.

The most important overseas market, the USA, was entered in 1957 with the sale of a carpet shearing machine to Walters Carpet Mill in California. It is fitting that, of all the machines available in the product range, it was a carpet shear which opened this market. Sellers manufacture the current undisputed market leader in carpet shearing machines- the 'Horizon'. Its success is unrivalled throughout the whole carpet industry.

Back-up service and spare part availability is one of the Company's aims together with an ability to deliver on time. There is a highly skilled workforce and engineers are ready to travel with the minimum delay to carry out service visits regardless of which part of the world (Visas permitting)!

In the late 1960s Sellers & Company was sold to Mather & Platt which was itself taken over by the Australian Wormald International Group. In 1985, however a buy-out was led by managing director, David Armitage, re-establishing the independence of Sellers & Company.

Business has prospered since then. The new Board of Directors opened the Sellers Service Center in Dalton, Georgia, "capital" of the US carpet industry. Then, progressively, they invested in new buildings and modern machine tools.

Priority was given to Research and Development activities resulting in seven new machines being introduced in as many years. A dedicated Computer

Sellers & Company are proud of their international reputation as manufacturers of high quality and state of the art machinery.

Above: *The machine shop.*
Top: *The transportation department from the 1950s, an impressive fleet of vehicles with the commercial vans dressed in the distinctive livery of the company.*

Great Grandfather had a wheelbarrow

After the lean times of the 19th century, by 1870 Huddersfield was beginning to thrive with commercial activity. Ben Shaw sensed that the time was favourable to leave the textile industry and embark on a joint venture with his brother George. In 1871 they set up 'Shaw Bros, Manufacturers of Non-alcoholic Beverages.

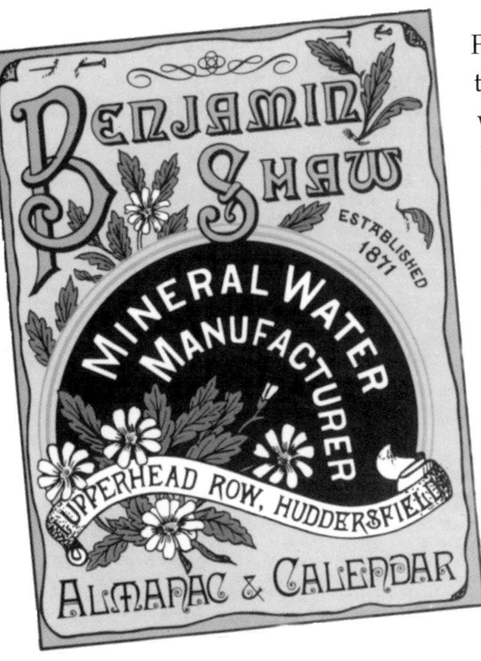

Five years later, the partnership was dissolved. Ben paid George £317 13s 6d and became sole owner of the business of which he was the inspiration. According to an extant receipt John Wardle of Manchester gave Ben "instruction in the manufacture of Porter (Botanic)" at a cost of £5. For six pounds he acquired "one horse and gears", three pounds on account and the rest some months later. Money was obviously tight.

Ben was keenly interested in public affairs, standing for and being elected to the Borough Council as an Independent member. He is known to have made forceful and useful contributions to debates.

He was prominent in the Mineral Water Manufacturers Association and glowing tributes were made about him in their trade journal.

Elms Yard in Charles Street was the site of Ben's first 'manufactory'. There, peculiarly shaped bottles were filled with Horehound Beer and Botanic Porter.

Various records and the original wheelbarrow still survived from the earliest years and the business expanded rapidly. Twelve years later a move was made to larger premises in Upperhead Row at the Westgate Corner and, less than a decade after that this factory too had become too small. Ben rented a town office and became one of the pioneer telephone users in Huddersfield, his number being 383.

Willow Lane

Ben's decision to erect a large, purpose-built factory was far-sighted and courageous. The wooded outskirts of Huddersfield that he chose were ideal for the manufacture of mineral waters. He had a water main specially laid so that he could use the water from the Pennines which had already proved exceptional at Upperhead Row. Pipes of 'pure block tin' passed through a 'patent rectifier' and powerful filters.

Motor wagons were introduced, the first one in 1905, which gradually took over from horses, whilst the buildings were continually extended.

In 1997 the top floor was converted into modern offices and state-of-the-art production facilities were installed. Today only one of the original offices remains. It is the old private office with the stand-up desk in front of the window and the partners' desk in the middle of the floor.

The factory was an early example of flow-production layout. Cases and empty bottles came in at one end of the factory. In sequence they were washed, sterilised, filled, labelled, boxed and stacked on the loading stage at the despatch end. Nine decades later, the basis of these facilities is still in situ.

The factory Ben was rightly proud of seems quaintly primitive today. It is just within living memory that small runs of less popular flavours were hand-syrupped on a four-ladle dipper. Quite soon the original machinery was replaced with more modern and efficient facilities.

Above: *The Willow Lane factory in 1978 with the original factory in the background.* ***Top:*** *The Willow Lane factory some ninety years ago.* ***Left:*** *The transport fleet of 1950 arrayed in Willow Lane.* ***Facing page, top left:*** *This calendar would have been given to customers and suppliers at the turn of the century.* ***Facing page, top right:*** *Benjamin Shaw, founder of the company.* ***Facing page, bottom left:*** *A delivery wagon. Incidentally, when this photograph was taken the horse, Bonny was retiring. This was her last load.*

That Ben's first registered trade mark was a dandelion plant indicates that drinks were based on roots. As his products developed, a mark with a more general significance was called for. Twenty years later, he registered 'Amicus Humani Generis' (Friend of the Human Race.) Today, the firm still uses the trade mark on its products.

Shaws' bottles have been collectors' items for some time. The best-remembered is the 'Codd' bottle with the glass poppy in its neck. They were difficult to fill and clean and are now rarely seen since they were often broken by small boys to obtain the marble.

Following the instincts of their founder, the company was the first independent manufacturer to can soft drinks in great Britain. Today, the factory produces over forty million litres of spring water a year. This is drawn from the borehole which was sunk in the 1930s and sourced from the finest spring water which has permeated through the Pennines for over sixty years. The company has also developed into the third largest dispense company of soft drinks in Great Britain and is now a member of Rutland Trust PLC.

Above: *The private office is all that remains of the original structure.* ***Top:*** *Round the corner from Charles Street, the environment of the first factory looking towards Upperhead Mills in 1939.*

The 'Yorkshire' treatment for the world's fibres

Albion Mill was built in 1864 but, during recent building work which involved excavation of part of the site, evidence of a substantial earlier building was discovered some metres below current ground level. At this lower level a stream also runs, now encased in a stone built culvert. It is apparent that manufacturing has been carried out on the site for more than 150years but unfortunately there are no records which give details.

R. Butterworth & Son Ltd. was established here in 1950, though the family had bought the business from the previous owners in 1946. Mr. Ronald Butterworth had worked for John Woodheads at a spinning mill in Thongsbridge.

He was a cousin of the Woodheads. His son, Mr. Brian Butterworth, had fought in the Army in Europe before joining his father in setting up his enterprise in Albion Mill.

He learned the wool-spinning trade, as did many at the time, at Huddersfield Technical College. Mr. Brian Butterworth's son Jonathan is the current chairman and managing director, supported by a highly skilled team of technicians and craftsmen and women. The company's business, since its foundation has been woollen spinning.

In latter years the emphasis has been on ever finer yarns for both the knitting and weaving trades. High class yarns are manufactured using the best raw materials available, bought from local merchants or imported.

The company buys fine lambswool from Australia, cashmere from China and Mongolia, silk and angora from China and other speciality fibres from countries worldwide.

Butterworth's use conventional woollen processing machinery of either British or European manufacture, enhanced these days in key areas with computer control.

Some machinery, where appropriate, has been renewed

many times to follow progress. However, because of the gentle treatment that the finest materials need to enhance their luxurious nature, older and slower equipment, provided it receives the scrupulous maintenance that Butterworths give it, cannot be beaten.

Over the years the company's products have been sold into the world's markets. Today though, the concentration is in the home market. The yarns

manufactured in Meltham can be found in the better high street stores throughout the land and in the most upmarket fashion houses around the world.

Many of the company's customers export a large proportion of their production into markets as far apart as Japan and America using Butterworth yarns.

Butterworths are renowned as highly flexible suppliers to the marketplace, selling both large volume products for the big industrial knitters and weavers and small-scale speciality yarns for the

high value end of the trade, using the finest and most expensive raw materials. The company well understands that continued success will depend on continuing to provide the high level of service and quality that have made its reputation.

Above: *An atmospheric view of Albion Mill, home of Butterworths since 1950.*
Centre: *Christmas 1938 saw the workforce of Butterworths at a party. It is hard to imagine that many of the men featured in the photograph would soon be donning army uniforms and fighting for their lives on foreign soil.*
Facing page, bottom left: *Albion Mill taken from a slightly elevated angle from a much earlier period than the picture above although nothing has changed very much over the years.*
Below: *The modern premises at Albion Mills, Meltham, Huddersfield.*

F. Drake & Company - a dream realised

At the age of 40, Joshua Drake dreamed of establishing a family firm. Possibly feeling he had left it rather late for himself, or perhaps as a pledge to the future, he named his enterprise 'F. Drake' after his three year old son Frank.

The company was registered in 1887 and there has been a continuous family association since then with its business of processing and selling natural and synthetic fibres.

In the nineteenth century, the fibre was, of course, all natural. In 1887, Victoria Mills was divided into units. (Is there anything new?) Joshua Drake began by renting a unit for pulling flocks - much used in pillow filling. He employed his two much younger brothers, Fred aged 23 and John William aged 20, in recycling discarded textile-fabrics. Fred invested in the company too and business prospered. Before long, both Joshua's sons were taken on.

Above: *Fred Drake, one of the founders of F. Drake & Co.*
Top: *An artist's impression of Manor Mill as it was in 1927.*
Right: *The company has always shown interest in horses. Jim checks a load to be delivered by Molly in 1968.*

When Joshua died the remaining members of the family widened the scope of the business. Manor Mills were purchased and the company began sorting, grading and garnetting, ready to sell to the cloth manufacturers in the Batley area. The fabric blends they produced were bought for soldiers' uniforms during the first world war.

Fred continued to run the firm but Frank and Harry were both called up and both of them were killed in enemy action. Percy Drake, Fred's son came to work with him and had to take charge after Fred's sudden death in 1925. Percy continued the rag pulling and garnetting work supplying the woollen manufacturers of the Colne Valley. In 1960 two old

Golcar families fully involved on all sides of the cloth trade, had cause to celebrate. James Haigh, son of Beaumont & Sarah Haigh, married Christine Muriel Drake, Percy & Sally's youngest daughter.

In 1965 James & Christine took over the Company and James, finding he was a natural entrepreneur, transformed the old trade into a modern progressive endeavour. New machinery was installed to deal with the modern synthetic materials, nylon, terylene, and crimplene.

In 1972, a subsidiary company, primarily owned by F Drake & Company of Golcar Ltd. was formed to produce polypropylene fibre for the spinning industry. This off-shoot venture, F Drake (Fibres) Ltd, was subsequently sold to Readicut International plc. in 1986.

***Top:** A family picture with Joshua Drake at the back, in the centre.*
***Above:** Jim and Christine Haigh with father Percy and Grandfather Fred Drake in the photograph in the background.*

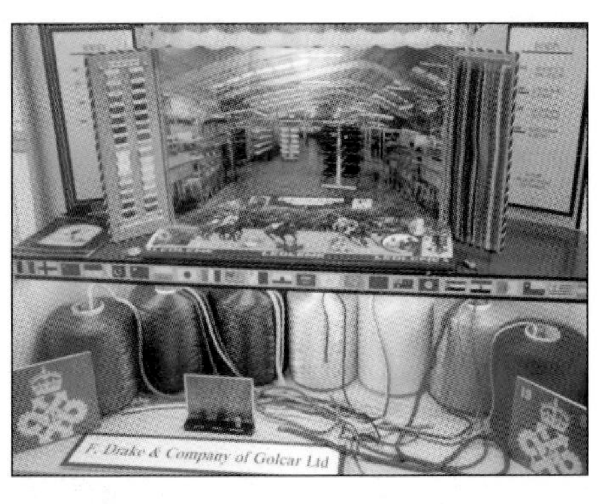

James Haigh re-invested the proceeds of this sale and built a new mill in Slaithwaite on the Spafield Industrial Estate. This was the first new mill to be built in the upper Colne Valley for 40 years. Begun in 1986, the 5 million pound plant was operational by the following year.

Under the umbrella of Jim Haigh's firm guidance The Queen's Award for Export Achievement was granted in 1981, and again in 1988.

The next generation has brought in Joshua, who with his father James and their company's team, constantly update machinery and are deeply involved in development and innovation so as to be in the

Above: *A display of Leolene, the firm's product, at a trade fair in Frankfurt. The Queen's Award for Export, won by the company in 1988, is shown on either side of the display.*
Left: *Sir Cyril Smith demonstrating the strength of Leolene yarn (he weighed 28 stone at the time). The event was G. MEX in September 1987.*
Below: *Lord Ingrow, flanked by Christine and Jim Haigh, presents the Queen's Award for Industry (Export) in 1988 at the Slaithwaite factory.*

forefront of technology. Another wholly owned company J & J Haigh has been formed.

With six huge silos and a hundred thousand square feet of floor space, the company has a vastly increased production. Technical advances and state-of-the-art machinery allows them to manufacture at low cost but at increased strength. The yarn is ideal for lifting straps, small ropes and sports netting. It is used for hay nets, girths and head collars for horses and even Post Office bags.

LEOLENE, has all the properties of an inert substance. That means it is resistant to water and chemicals. It will float and so is useful for ships' ropes.

F Drake & Company of Golcar Ltd has always taken its responsibility to the community seriously. The Haigh family works hard for local charities and assists local groups through sponsorship. For the last 20 years the company has staged annually a charity polo match at Toulston Polo ground near Tadcaster, which raised £30,000 in 1997 for a variety of Charities. They also sponsor the Drake's Huddersfield and district cricket league which encourages young players in local teams.

Support is given to fledgling entrepreneurs through the Prince's Youth Business Trust which gives practical guidance to young people in business. Jim & Joshua are active members of the Polyolefin Textile Association and the European Association for Textile Polyolefins. Jim Haigh is a past president of the Huddersfield Textile Society.

Business is never easy but F Drake & Company of Golcar is confident about the future, having a past that has been built up on a willingness to face the future with courage, innovation and hands-on responsibility. Their motto is reflected by the words of the hymn FORWARD EVER FORWARD.

Above: *Advertising Leolene, the company product. Christine M. Haigh presenting the Queen's Silver Jubilee Plate to the winner at their charity polo match in 1997.*
Top: *F. Drake & Company of Golcar Ltd sponsored the Careers Resource Centre of Colne Valley High School at the opening on 25th September 1996. Jim and Christine Haigh (on the left) are with the Headmaster Alan Newton, the Chairman of the Governors, John Scott and the Deputy Mayor and Mayoress, Cllr. Heather Swift and Margaret Fearnley.*

Frank Platt - the electrical pioneer with a promising future

The history of Frank Platt Electrical Ltd dates back to the earliest 'wireless', back in 1928 with the founder himself at South Lane, Holmfirth.

Frank Platt learned his trade whilst working as a foreman in charge of 26 engineers, in the employ of Charles Tolson, Holmfirth and in 1928 he had acquired the expertise to set up on his own. Local textile mills needed updating to modern electrical standards and Platt's played their part in this endeavour.

During this period Frank Platt decided that the 'wireless' looked like taking off and opened his shop on South Lane. In those days a wireless could cost as much as £23 and more electrical appliances came onto the market to fill his new adventure. But, as before his main passion still remained on electrical installations. In 1936 the retailing arm grew and new, larger premises had to be sought. The shop then moved 500 yards to Market Walk, next to the Valley Theatre, Holmfirth, where business carried on until the outbreak of the Second World War in 1939.

During the war, Mr Platt worked on highly secret munitions work, electronics being his expertise. He would be collected early Monday mornings and not return until late the following Saturday. The business had to carry on without him.

After the war, Frank Platt with the gradual decline in the local textile industry, which unfortunately meant a slow down in work generated within the trade. Retailing work slowly took over.

Although he had little interest in retailing, his eldest son Robert, was starting in the business and saw retailing as the way forward.

After success in Holmfirth, the following years saw branches open in Penistone (1953) and Stocksbridge (1956).

The first colour television set the company sold had a 23" screen and cost 349 guineas (it was delivered in a new Morris-Minor van costing £495!) and over the

Above: *Frank Platt, the founder standing proudly outside his shop in February 1928 on South Lane, Holmfirth.*
Left: *Frank Platts' premises in Market Walk to where the company moved in 1936.*